Advance praise for *Soulfull*

"I haven't met Farrell Mason yet, but when I do, I'll greet her with a hug and great gratitude. *Soulfull* rebuilt and bolstered some corners of my soul that had been worn away over the last couple of years, and I can't wait to press it into the hands of so many people I love who are similarly tired, hungry, and scraped away on a soul level. What a gift!"
—Shauna Niequist, *New York Times* bestselling author of
I Guess I Haven't Learned That Yet

"Cooking, walking, listening to music—we're doing that stuff anyway, right? We might as well claim it all as special. Farrell Mason is showing us how to do just that in *Soulfull*. She suggests that life is magic because we decide it is, simple as that. What a gem of a book."
—Jen Hatmaker, *New York Times* bestselling author of
Feed These People

"This book will not only fill you up with joy but draw you in with hope. You are going to be inspired by the practical and engaging adventure Farrell Mason has invited you on. Buckle up—you are going to love this book and will find yourself sharing the simple truths and creative content with your friends!"
—Bob Goff, *New York Times* bestselling author of *Everybody, Always*

Soulfull

Soulfull

A Weekly Devotional to Nourish the Mind, Body, and Spirit

Farrell Mason

Convergent
New York

Published in the United States by Convergent Books, an imprint of Random House, a division of Penguin Random House LLC, New York.

CONVERGENT BOOKS is a registered trademark and the Convergent colophon is a trademark of Penguin Random House LLC.

Hardback ISBN 978-0-593-44415-3
Ebook ISBN 978-0-593-44416-0

Printed in Canada

convergentbooks.com

2 4 6 8 9 7 5 3

Book design by Virginia Norey
Title page and chapter opener art from Tonia Tkach/stock.adobe.com

FOR

Duke, my wild and crazy dad, who taught me by example that family, faith, nature, food, adventure, laughter, and contributing to the greater good was the recipe for living a meaningful life.

Lovey and David, you are the reason my center holds.

Charlie, Belle, Elise, Rose, Percy, and Finn, you make up the sacred and wildly adventurous liturgy of my life.

Listen to your life. See it for the fathomless mystery that it is. In the boredom and pain of it, no less than in the excitement and gladness; touch, taste, smell your way to the holy and hidden part of it, because in the last analysis all moments are key moments, and life itself is grace.

—FREDERICK BUECHNER

I have come that they may have life, and have it to the full.

—JOHN 10:10 (NIV)

Contents

Introduction

Welcome to a Year of Living Soulfully.

This book came to life when a question kept nudging me for an answer: "Am I living the life I want to live?" The honest answer was, *sometimes.* Certainly not always. Sitting in the pew at a young friend's funeral, I realized I operated my life on the premise that there would always be more time. I see now how short the earthly stay truly is. I have to be more intentional with how I wish to live what the poet Mary Oliver calls "[my] one wild and precious life."

Intellectually, more importantly, spiritually—I know the life I want to live: a loving, creative, and adventurous one; lower in stress and family centered; enriched with meaningful relationships and guided by a true and evolving faith; to approach the future not in fear, but with a healthy curiosity for all the possibilities. Faced with likely struggles, I do not want to shrink—I want to expand.

As a mother of six, a pastoral minister, and an author, most of my days are spent flying by the seat of my pants. I can easily become lost in the whirl. My own life is accepted imperfection. Experience has taught me that. I know both the beautiful and the tragic. My first son was treated for stage 4 cancer and then I crazily, miraculously had five more children! My house is more Grand Central Station than monastery. I love to cook, but I also burn a lot of dishes. For me, bliss is a lavender Epsom salt bath—until you forget you left the water running and it floods your bathroom and your daughter's bedroom ceiling below collapses. One moment I am dealing with teenage shenanigans and helping with college applications, and the next, I am teaching a younger one how to tie his shoes and read Dr. Seuss. My six-year-old son sometimes has a sailor's mouth. He's got two older brothers! I am a working mother, which means there are days when I am less than sunshine. Visit my house any day of the week, and you will find laundry stacked to the ceiling. My heart has been broken by family and friends, and vice versa. I would be lying if I didn't confess that unholy words can be said in trying to get my family to church on Sunday mornings.

I love God. I love people. I love nature. There are times when I doubt God. I sometimes love my pets more than people. And nature scares me. I am afraid of the throw-up bug, lice, and, more than I would like to admit, pain and death. Sometimes I read the Bible and pray, sometimes I do not. But through it all, I know this: **Imperfect lives can be holy.** I continue to be grateful for the chance to participate. And I am trying my best to make it a soulfull adventure.

The parental and work responsibilities, the losses and setbacks, along with society's challenges of secularity and technology, and the existential fears that come with just being human—all try to thwart my soulfull desires. No wonder Jesus calmly told his disciples, "Stay awake."* He knew how easily the sacred thread can slip through our mortal fingers. I need regular soul wake-up calls, words of encouragement, and sometimes even a grab by the proverbial collar to make me straighten up and seek a

* Matthew 24:42, ESV

more sacred existence, one that is wide, consequential, and flushed with joy. Maybe you're seeking some of the same things too.

So, how can we regularly experience the soulfullness we crave? It is a daily mission to participate from the best within us. We must commit to discovering creative ways to pull a bit of heaven down to our patches of earth. To do this we have to slow down, reflect, adapt gracefully to change, include more of the good, and subtract the unnecessary. We must rise when knocked down, pray, forgive, make peace, have hope, and take care of our health and the health of those we love. For me, this is the fun part—a lifelong journey.

The adventure will not always be sweet, but it can always be sacred. The universe is asking us to open our arms to every encounter, relationship, defeat, success, hope, and dream. Bravery is required. The goal is to live a life of deep meaning colored by its joy. *Soulfull* is a gentle guide to a deeper, more fulfilled human spiritual experience: through time spent in nature, in humble prayer and honest reflection, in food and fellowship, and especially in contributing to the greater good of others and our planet.

Soulfull is an invitation to nourish your mind, body, and spirit to discover a more sacred, joy-filled, and hope-giving life.

My hope in writing *Soulfull* is to meet you where you are and fill up your unique soul. The goal is to embrace a new sacred rhythm, one that will invite more wonder, delight, and peace. Use the book as a weekly devotional or as a guide to create your own soulfull adventure.

In these pages you'll find fifty-two reflections, prayers, and souljoy activities to nourish your mind, body, and spirit, and welcome a more sacred existence.

Spiritual Reflections

THE LONGING TO live a life that matters requires a sacred commitment that begins in our **minds**. Each week, you will be encouraged by an inspiring quote, a meaningful Bible verse, and

a spiritual homily to support that commitment. These reflections tackle all the things we experience on Earth: the evolution of ourselves, the understanding and expansion of our experiences of God, relationships with fellow human beings (how wonderful and challenging that can be), the meeting of disappointment and loss with resilience, and the awareness and attention to our flaws and limitations. This is a lifelong endeavor to be more than just happy, but to be soulfilled with a joy that lights us from the inside out.

Prayers

THROUGH OUR SPIRITS, we are connected to a divine reality greater than ourselves. We are invited to lean into God for counsel, understanding, hope, and forgiveness. We were never meant to do this human project on our own. And my need for God is not unique. The weekly prayers I've included are written in the first person because I believe the conversation between the human heart and God is personal. Much like the Psalms, my prayers reflect every human emotion and yearning. I hope that by reading them, you will be encouraged to try your own.

Souljoys

EACH WEEK INCLUDES an action item to activate our connection to our **bodies** and physically live out the soulfull experience. You will be encouraged to try many things, such as creating a private altar in your home or a natural environment, adopting a simple meditation practice, or making scented oils. Some weeks offer a simple walk in nature to welcome self-reflection and dreaming. Other weeks encourage listening to music to uplift your spirit. For me, my soul becomes radiant when I tie on an apron, put a soup pot on the stove, and have family pull up chairs around my kitchen table. So, twenty-two of these souljoys are my original family-favorite recipes that are simple to prepare, healthy, and nourishing to the body as well as the soul.

My hope is that *Soulfull* will be like one of my most beloved cookbooks that sits front and center on the kitchen counter for inspiration, well-used with many earmarked pages and spaghetti-sauce fingerprints. This is my encyclopedia of hope, a place to find light in the darkness. *Soulfull* is your invitation to take a sacred pause to reflect, renew, and begin again. Feel free to dip in and out, taking what you need each week to encourage your own soulfull experience. Count on some serendipities as you open to a week and find it was exactly what you needed in that moment. I also created a "Resources for Living Soulfully" index in the back for those days when you need a reflection, activity, or recipe to meet the season you are in. What you will not find is a guide to a perfect life. Just roll up your sleeves and get your hands in the dirt, embracing life in all its complexity and beauty—which can be messy. The reward, however, is an unforgettable journey that shines with meaning and radiates joy.

Let's begin by taking an accounting of our lives. Let's take some time and do a self check-in, asking ourselves these questions and considering the current state of our souls.

- What brings us joy? What does not?
- Where and when do we feel especially peaceful and balanced? When do we not?
- What is holding us back from becoming who we would like to be? What can we let go of to make room for something better?
- How do we cope with setbacks? Do we practice daily resilience?
- Do our relationships nourish or diminish us? Do we offer unconditional love to our significant others?
- What resentments and hurts can we sweep from our inner house, to finally be free?
- Does our spiritual life bring us comfort and enrich our earthly life?
- Are we people of hope? Are we building and rebuilding our inner reserves of hope?

Welcome to the beautiful and worthy work of living soulfully.

Soulfull

1

Build Your Nest

I want to think again of dangerous and noble things. I want to be
light and frolicsome. I want to be improbable beautiful and afraid
of nothing, as though I had wings.
—MARY OLIVER

They will be like a tree planted by the water that sends out its roots by
the stream. It does not fear when heat comes; its leaves are always
green. It has no worries in a year of drought and never fails to bear fruit.
—JEREMIAH 17:8 (NIV)

It was an exciting discovery that a pair of young eagles had chosen the
lake a mile from my house to build their first nest and start a family.
These magnificent birds stand two feet tall with a wingspan nearly the
length of my old Suburban. Bald eagles mate for life and spend their entire
life span constructing an exquisite nest. Unlike other avian friends who
whip together a new nest each spring, bald eagles refine and expand theirs
with every passing season. A first-year eagle's nest measures six feet in
circumference. After twenty years, this work of art exhibiting amazing
creativity, determination, and faith nearly triples in size and weighs over
a ton.

On a morning jog around Radnor Lake near my home in Nashville, I
witnessed the male eagle proudly soaring over the lake with a six-foot
branch in his talons (eagles can carry half their weight) to buttress his architectural marvel. Later that month, I saw a watch party had gathered
around with a high-powered lens to film the newlywed eagles traversing

the lake while clutching bright green moss, fern, and feathers to improve their masterpiece of a dwelling.

It is our lifelong mission and adventure to build a meaningful existence.

I am disillusioned by how our culture defines a successful life. Many are celebrated for having "made it," but in settling for mile-wide, inch-deep lives, they can feel empty and full of regret. The key is learning how to live in the world without losing yourself to it. The silver lining of the COVID-19 pandemic was that many of us were awakened to the gap between the way we were living our daily lives and the lives our souls craved. An internal reckoning began as we realized nobody wants to wake up one day and have missed the real purpose in life.

Arthur Brooks, a social scientist, author, and professor at Harvard Business School, has dedicated his life's work to studying what makes human beings truly happy. He says that culture tells us to love things, use people, and worship ourselves. **Our souls tell us the exact opposite.** Beautiful lives happen when we use things, love people, and worship the Divine. Before there were ladders to climb, promotions to score, reputations to seal, and bank accounts to fill, we had a soul, holy and with divine purpose. Ask yourself, what is holy about your existence? Are you a person only of the world? Or does your soul direct you to another path?

In other words, are you content with the nest you are building?

If not careful, we can spend the bulk of our days secretly dissatisfied, lost, and blue—smaller versions of ourselves. But a Jewish friend of mine once said, "If you eat life from your soul, you will be full." A helpful guide is to construct one's nest with spiritual materials that will not turn to dust: a morning walk in nature, the embrace of a child or lover, an evening of delicious food and laughter, moments of quiet and reflection absent of technology, regular soul-baring conversations with God, and many, many acts of kindness.

One activity for the soul a day is a worthy goal. Expect a more sacred existence.

The eagles of Radnor Lake cannot predict nor control what tomorrow holds. Neither can we. Each year, each season, brings new challenges and rewards, losses, and gains. The eagles' and our days are numbered in the Book of Life. The time is now to feather our nests with the things that truly matter.

God,

Love me into
who You know I can be,
a creative and
benevolent energy.
A prophet, a healer,
a fount of mercy,
a saving grace.

I am slow in my evolving,
stumbling in contradiction,
but ever hopeful that with You,
the Infinite can be revealed
in the finite of me.

Love realized—
My soul wondrously full.

Amen.

Nest-Building Tips to Create a Soulfull Life

TIME IS PRECIOUS. I am determined more than ever to squeeze all the nectar from this human experience. My soul wants more, and I believe yours does too. All we need to live the soulfull life is an open heart, a curious and resilient spirit, and a daily desire to live our best life. Following are six nest-building tips to get your foundation started.

Number 1: Spend Time in Nature

Put yourself regularly in the path of beauty. A good start is time spent in the mountains, by the ocean, in a forest or nearby park, or in your own backyard. The Bible opens in a garden and closes in a garden for a reason. Jesus chooses nature as a place to teach, to speak to God, to eat, to pray, to bless, to heal, to perform miracles, and to refresh himself for the demands of his mortal life. Nature reveals to us so much about God. The greenness, the blueness, the warmth of the sun, the coolness of the shade—all heal, even save us, one vignette of beauty at a time. When the world is too much, find a square inch of green and reset. As they say in Jackson Hole, Wyoming, "Bring the outside in." Find an evergreen chapel and open yourself to the sacred.

Number 2: Build and Rebuild Relationships

Engagements with other human beings expose flaws, insecurities, and fragility. In the same breath, they can reveal the best in us and in others. Victor Hugo wrote in *Les Misérables* that our interactions with fellow human beings allow us to "see the face of God." Mend, forgive, encourage, nurture, and sacrifice for the relationships that matter to us. Walk in another's shoes to know where he or she has been and desperately hopes to be going. Take in all of this information and then sincerely engage. The goal is fewer duels and more prodigal homecomings.

Number 3: Break Bread Together

Something transcendent happens around the table. When we pull up the chairs, light the candles, and serve family, friends, and even strangers a roasted chicken, homemade pesto pasta, or a peach cobbler—what we are actually serving is love, mercy, and hope. Souls are being fed.

Number 4: Find Your Purpose and Go After It

Souljoy is found by going after something—a dream, a relationship, a passion. It might be cooking, writing, counseling, gardening, painting, parenting, singing, or inventing. The mission is to endeavor a life that is layered, colorful, and shining with meaning. Make your unique experience unforgettable.

Number 5: Grow and Evolve

Pablo Picasso said, "We don't grow older, we grow riper." Forget the age number! We are here to discover who we are and all we can be. Participate in many personal resurrections over a lifetime. Fail and then rise. Then do it again. Believe that something beautiful can be born and reborn from brokenness. Live in expectation of what marvelous thing God will do next in your life.

Number 6: Fall in Love

St. John of the Cross said, "In the evening of life, we will be judged on love alone." Make it your life's mission to fall in love with people, places, experiences, nature, yourself—but especially with God.

2

Finding Eden

Paradise is at your own center. Unless you find it there,
there is no way to enter.
—ANGELUS SILESIUS

The kingdom of God is within you.
—LUKE 17:21 (ASV)

In a small hilltop village in the southwest of France, where my family has visited over the last twenty years, there is a conclave of lovely old houses tucked behind stone and iron gates dating back to the eighteenth century. One special house sits in the center of a grove of ancient olive trees; another is surrounded by thick cedar hedges clipped in geometric forms. Each house is identified not by numbers but by pleasing names: *Mas du Fer à Cheval* (House of the Horseshoe), *Bastide du Bonheur* (Country House of Happiness), *Mas des Anges* (House of Angels), and *Mas de la Chouette* (House of the Owl). One in particular speaks to me—it is simply called Eden.

Fragrant jasmine entwines its gates, and an enormous cherry tree beckons with its early blossoms. The aroma of fresh morning bread perfumes the air, and one can hear the bees buzzing cheerfully around rows of lavender. An adorable white Scottish terrier with a red bandana tied around his neck is a sentry at the gate, barking a happy *bonjour* to all who pass. I have a recurring dream of slipping past the gate and entering this lovely paradise.

Deep down, don't we all long for this—Eden? I am not speaking of a geographic location—the isles of Fiji or New Zealand nor a hilltop village in France—but an interior oasis, a spiritual state of being that extends out into our day-to-day lives, lending a benevolent vision of the world.

The idea of Eden is always beckoning us. But more often than we would like, we only peek through the gate, instead of making it the home for our souls. What a gift to glimpse Eden in this imperfect life, so frenetic, increasingly secular, materialistic, unpredictable, often unjust, and always much too short. Some try to create for themselves a self-made version of Eden with money, power, achievement, and indulgence. Eventually, all turns to dust right before their eyes.

Eden is not achieved, that is to say, arrived at; it is *experienced*. We encounter it as a mystical awareness that whatever might be happening *outside* us, a little of heaven is possible *within* us. Jesus says, "My peace I give you. I do not give to you as the world gives."* Eden is the encountering of that mysterious peace only God can give us.

I can make the journey in and out of Eden in a single thought. The moment I lose my sense of wonder and gratitude for my life, I'm out of Eden. The moment I allow bitterness to rule my thoughts and actions: *I'm out.* The moment I let fear speak loudly over everything else in my life: *I'm out.* The moment I allow social media to substitute for real hugs and face-to-face "I love you"s: *I'm out.* The moment I choose the secular over the sacred, ignore the needs of my soul, push God to the fringes of my life (until I need something): *I'm out.* However, the moment I slow down, soften my edges, and take in the beauty around me: *I'm in.* The moment I forgive the one I have dragged my feet to forgive: *I'm in.* The

* John 14:27, NLV

moment I accept God's grace for myself: *I'm in.* The moment I love with all my heart: *I'm in.* The moment I lead from my truest self, my soul: *I'm in.* The moment I trust God with my today and tomorrow: *I'm in.*

Eden is within your grasp. No one is in control of your life but you. Your soul is whispering to you the way. Welcome quiet, because the soul is attuned to a different wavelength, subtle and otherworldly, that runs below the blaring noise of our material world. Just know that inside the stone gates of our earthly lives, an inner sanctuary is possible where God offers our souls true peace, absolute truth, and a chance for wholeness.

Spend this year discovering Eden and living more often from this peaceful place.

Holy One,

Why me,
Why here?

To fall in love,
with myself, with my clan,
with the pileated woodpecker dressed in a
crimson-plumed headdress,
and especially with You, God.

To manifest in my unique way a spark of the Divine
in my time and space.
To reveal that I am more than dust,
I am a soul.

To accomplish something worthy with the soft muscle
of my heart.
To slip a word of hope into every conversation.
To be a tuning fork, maybe help work a miracle or two.

To duel with fear and walk away champion.
To remember the last always goes first, the servant
before the crown,
and humbly take my place in line.

To be a wellspring of peace.
First, finding it within,
nurturing it.
Then, breathing it out into the world.

To become a gourmand of grace,
tie my apron about me,
use every pot and pan in my cupboard,
set a table beautiful for a multitude,
and spend my life nourishing souls.

To take every "glory" experience,
even the ones that break my heart
and allow them to transform me
into Your emissary of love,
and ambassador of hope.

Amen to that!

An Invitation to Access Your Personal Eden by Praying with Beads

A FULLNESS OF soul requires regular quiet and whispered prayers. Praying with beads is an ancient Christian spiritual practice. It invites a sense of calm, inner focus, and a deeper experience of God and the spiritual Eden within and all around us. Using a string of beads, a bracelet of prayer beads, or a rosary, follow these seven invitations to speak the longings of your heart.

Start by enclosing the beads in the palm of your hand, close your eyes, take a deep breath, and say, "God be with me." Now, move your finger across each bead and recite each prayer below either aloud or silently. Savor the quiet and the moving meditation through the beads. You may repeat the litany as many times as you like. You may also choose a Psalm from the Bible and move your finger across each bead corresponding with a line from the Psalm, or you may assign a bead for a specific person, circumstance, or petition.

Bead One: Loving God, I give you thanks that I can speak my heart and know that whatever the current circumstances, however long it has been since I have reached out to You, You are here with me, as close as my heartbeat and as near as my breath. I am never alone.

Bead Two: Loving God, I pray for a dose of the peace only You can give. I long to feel soft and hopeful on the inside so that I can be a light to others.

Bead Three: Loving God, I pray for mercy for the times I have fallen short in love. Forgive my doubts and distance. Thank you for gifting me with another chance to leave a footprint of goodness.

Bead Four: Loving God, I pray for courage to trust You in all circumstances, with all that I am and love, my today and tomorrow. There is a beautiful and redemptive plan unfolding in my life and across creation. You promise it. I just need Your help trusting it. Help me pray the ultimate words of faith: Thy will be done.

Bead Five: Loving God, I pray for all the seen and unseen places in my life that reveal my fragility. Make me more than well in mind, body, and spirit so that I may fulfill Your design for my life. However dark the night, please let the joy return in the morning!

Bead Six: Loving God, I ask humbly for what this world cannot give me: wonder, mystery, resurrection, surprises of grace—heaven.

Bead Seven: Loving God, I pray that today You would help me live a life that matters, one that increases love in the world and radiates joy.

3

Live in Hope

Our mission is to plant ourselves at the gates of Hope.
—VICTORIA SAFFORD

We have this hope, a sure and steadfast anchor of the soul, a hope that
enters the inner shrine behind the curtain.
—HEBREWS 6:19 (NRSV)

Barbara Brown Taylor, a priest, professor, and author of many bestselling books, is one of my spiritual heroes. She was in Nashville
speaking about her new book and afterward opened the floor to questions. I raised my hand and asked: "What is your definition of hope?"

Immediately, she bounced it back: "*You* tell me . . . what is hope?"

I felt a teenager's blush starting in my cheeks, and my palms quickly
dampened. I looked around the room and noticed three of my Vanderbilt
University Divinity School professors were there. I started to panic. It felt
like a movie—you know that moment where time stops and everyone is
frozen in place except for you? The scene darkened and the spotlight homed
in on me. Parnassus Bookshop was silent, everyone holding a breath for
my definition of hope. I closed my eyes and ordered my intellect, ego, and
theology to step aside. Trusting my heart to speak for me, I answered:

"God has me, whatever happens. Ultimately, all will be well.
There is a plan where God is making all things right and new."

Barbara Brown Taylor smiled and softly said, "Yes. Thank you."
What I realized later, and what she had known all along, was that I

had to answer the question for myself. The same is true for you. We must each answer the question "What is hope?" for ourselves. The answer is inside us.

Paul reminds us, "This hope is a strong and trustworthy anchor for our souls. It leads us through the curtain into God's inner sanctuary."* Beneath the skin—deeper than scars, sickness, disappointment, worries, and even fear of mortality—lives an eternal hope. It is in the marrow of us, written into our DNA. We are spiritually encoded to hope. Think for a holy minute. Every time we even hear the word *hope,* our spiritual antennae pick up the signal. Every cell in our bodies rises to attention.

Eighteen years ago, my firstborn son, Charlie, was diagnosed with stage 4 neuroblastoma cancer at only ten weeks old. I could not have told you with any certainty whether hope existed in that terrible, dark season of life. But flash forward eighteen years, and I know that hope was and is my superpower. It can become yours too. Hope carried me through my child's cancer, a miscarriage, several touch-and-go childbirths, delivering the painful eulogy for a dear friend who took his own life, and dozens more funerals for those I have loved and lost. This may surprise you, but I have felt hope strongest when sitting at the bedside of someone taking a last breath. Hope is responsible for every brave, beautiful, and redemptive vignette of my life. Few things I know for certain, but I do know this: There is always hope.

I find comfort in Lamentations—"And this is what I shall tell my heart and so recover hope: the favors of Yahweh are not all passed. His kindnesses are not exhausted. Every morning they are renewed. Great is his faithfulness."†

How, then, do you access the superpower of hope? Trust God, regard-

---

* Hebrews 6:19, NLT
† Lamentations 3:21–23, TJB

less of the circumstances. Surrender your will and expectations for desired outcomes and watch how God will far exceed your flagging hopes. Turn over your fears and disappointments, your present and your future, everything you are and love, even your death, to the One who loved you first, who will love you after and onward. In Jeremiah 29:11, God says, "I know the plans I have for you. Plans to prosper you and not to harm you, plans to give you hope and a future."*

A few years ago, I lived in London while attending graduate school. I discovered a painting at the Tate Gallery by George Frederic Watts entitled "Hope." It portrays hope to be not a sentiment but a choice. In the lovely work, a woman sits on top of a globe, and in her hand is a lute with all the strings broken except one. She plays the lone note with gusto.

Life is never going to be perfect or go exactly as you or I would like. And, of course, one day we will die. But until then, play your one string relentlessly, because as Paul assures us in his letter to the Romans, "suffering produces endurance; endurance, character; and character, hope. And hope does not disappoint."†

My simplest definition of hope: God is with me. Forever and always.

Dear Child of Mine,

As you go through this day, know that I am gently protecting you.
I am as near to you as your very breath, as close to you as your heartbeat.
I can see the fragile state of your emotions.

* NIV
† Romans 5:3–5, NET

I am aware that the wick of your spirit's inner light
is flickering
in the winds of your dilemma.
But you are my child, and I am on your side today,
and always.
I will hold you in my love until you are strong again.
Do not be troubled or afraid.
Do not strive in your own strength, but lean into
my love.
Be strengthened by my spirit.
Find comfort in my mercy.

—God

Chicken Soup

In a world where hope seems to be in short supply, nourish some-one's soul with a little homemade "hope." Make a love drop. Take my famous chicken soup and a mason jar of flowers, with the above "Dear Child of Mine" prayer enclosed, to a friend, family member, co-worker, or anyone whom you suspect could use a nudge of **hope**. There's a reason people call it "chicken soup for the soul"!

Ingredients

1 onion, diced
1 head of celery, diced
1 leek, diced
2 cups carrots, diced
1 bay leaf
2 tbsp herbes de Provence
1 tbsp dried oregano
salt and pepper
1 rind of Parmigiano-Reggiano
olive oil
1 whole organic chicken

1 cup cilantro, roughly chopped
1 cup Italian parsley, roughly
    chopped
1 cup basil, roughly chopped
2 cups fresh spinach, roughly
    chopped
2 cups brown rice
juice from 1 lime, for garnish
1 avocado, for garnish
1 cup Parmigiano-Reggiano, grated,
    for garnish

Directions

Combine onion, celery, leek, and carrots with bay leaf, herbes de Provence, oregano, salt, and pepper in your soup pot. Add rind of Parmigiano. Sauté in olive oil for 3–6 minutes, or until softened. Next, place your chicken in your soup pot and fill with water until chicken is covered. Allow to cook for an hour and a half. Once chicken is cooked through, turn off the heat, remove meat from bones, and return to the pot. Add cilantro, parsley, basil, and spinach. In a separate pot, prepare 2 cups brown rice and place in the bottom of each person's bowl, and then ladle in soup! Squeeze lime over soup and garnish with avocado and Parmigiano-Reggiano. This soup serves my family of 8, with generous leftovers for next day's lunch!

Bonus: As an added treat, sprinkle homemade croutons on top! Cut up big chunks of sourdough or olive bread; coat with olive oil, salt, and herbes de Provence; throw in the oven on broil for a few minutes; and then toss on top of the soup right before you serve. If I am delivering the soup, I wrap them up in tin foil. You can accompany the soup with a French baguette, grilled cheese sandwich, or cheese quesadillas (my kids' favorite!).

4

When Heaven Breaks Through

Beauty and grace are performed whether or not we will or sense
them. The least we can do is try to be there.
—Annie Dillard

I called to God from my narrowness,
and God answered me with a vast expanse.
—Psalm 118:5 (CJB)

There is no solving the issue of our finite existence. Aristotle suggested we not focus on "the end," but rather ways to flourish in the present. The American psychologist Abraham Maslov wrote about the necessity of having "peak experiences," where present reality is perceived as sublime, the brutal is forgotten for the beautiful, the ordinary radiates with transcendent meaning. To borrow from teenage jargon: Life gets a "glow-up"!

Transcendent moments hint of eternity. They offer a mystical awareness. The temporal falls away, and we are assured all will come together for good. These quicksilver episodes can happen in the presence of nature's astounding beauty or as witness to a miracle, and most often in powerful exchanges of love.

Spiritual mystics, especially in the Celtic tradition, speak of "thin places," where the sacred boundary of the unseen is breached and the veil between this world and heaven seems wondrously diaphanous. For a twinkling, we experience a deeper reality.

The thin places are not captured in a selfie. Nor are they scientifically proven by the Einsteins of the world. But the soul recognizes when something transcendent has transpired. Maybe you get goose bumps or spontaneously break into tears, your heart becomes lodged in your throat, or the hairs rise to attention on your arms. Maybe it occurs standing beneath a soaring majestic oak or listening to "Silent Night" on Christmas Eve, holding your newborn, or walking along the mighty ocean's edge, or just comes as a hint in that twilight moment right before you fall asleep. You might find yourself looking around for a witness, until you realize a Divine Presence has chosen this moment especially for you.

The poet Walt Whitman suggested a transcendent experience was possible through locating God in every hour. Theologically, I believe we are always in the presence of God. It is up to us to acknowledge the hope in the room. The church has a compelling repertoire for "pulling" heaven down to Earth. We light candles. We anoint our bodies with fragrant and healing oils. We sing canticles. We kneel and pray for life in abundance. And sometimes we feel the shimmer of the Spirit in our midst.

Every summer of my childhood, my family would load up our Suburban: six kids, two adults, a dog, a fish, sometimes a cat (Oreo had six kittens under my sister's bed one summer!), trunks full of clothes, and bags of jellybeans, and we'd head to the South Carolina coast. Without iPads or car TVs, we kiddos entertained ourselves with guessing the flavor of jellybeans until the bag was empty! As soon as we crossed the bridge onto the island of Kiawah, my dad would roll down all the windows so we could take our first big gulp of its salty-sweet air.

Almost a spiritual practice, I would carefully unbuckle each of my sandals and line them up on the boardwalk before stepping joyfully onto the beach. Even then, with my long hair twisted in braids, full of innocence, and grudgingly holding fast to one of my younger sisters' sticky hands, I felt reverence for the glory of that beautiful stretch of sandy beach and Carolina-blue sea. Curling my toes in the hot sand, I just knew in my child's heart that I was walking on holy ground.

God says to Moses, "Remove the sandals from your feet, because the place where you are standing is holy ground."* God asks Moses to recognize and honor the holiness within and all around him. I fear we rarely take off our sandals for anything in this day and age. Either too busy, self-absorbed, or jaded—we do not see the glory right in front of us.

The time is now to implement a spiritual practice of reverence. God is mercifully sitting on heaven's edge, waiting for us to discover the holiness everywhere and in everything.

Not long ago I sat at the bedside of my octogenarian friend who was very ill. She happily told me she wasn't afraid of death because for nearly a century, she had kept a detailed accounting of each time she had witnessed heaven here on Earth. She said, "You would be surprised how thin the boundary truly is between Earth and heaven, between God and you, if your eyes and heart are open to seeing it."

The secret to the art of transcendence is simple: Seek God's face always. Fall in love with the life given and keep falling in love over and over again—with people, nature, food, new experiences, and music. Be magnanimous often. Believe, believe, believe that a corner of heaven can be pulled down on your watch.

God of Love,

Today I will take my sandals off,
quiet the noise,

---

* Acts 7:33, CSB

> show fear the door,
> open my eyes to the wondrous,
> and just maybe,
> touch the hem of Your Robe.
>
> Never have I ever known what tomorrow holds,
> And I have spent time in the belly of the whale,
> but You never left me there for long,
> so why should I doubt You now?
> Your grace is embroidered into everything.
>
> Remind me again of Your promise:
> Even when all is not well and okay,
> all will be well and okay.
>
> Let heaven break through.
>
> Amen.

Music Invites Transcendence

THE FIRST TIME I experienced Antonio Vivaldi's "The Four Seasons" was in a candlelit chapel. I felt I had left my body and been transported to heaven's door. Music is a gift. God reveals the eternal in its marvelous notes.

In 1725, Vivaldi gifted the world with his opus, "The Four Seasons": four violin concertos, each representing one of the seasons. His avant-garde masterpiece is an example of tonal painting, where the orchestra brings to life sensory experiences in nature and human experience while also communicating deeper artistic and theological meanings. For Vivaldi, the whole of life was sacred and presented unlimited inspiration for joyous music compositions. He spent his life building metaphorical cathedrals with his music, where the beauty in creation and the presence of God could be grasped.

Music has the remarkable ability to transport us to another realm. You, too, can feel your spirit levitating within your human frame. Find a quiet place and listen to one of these songs, letting the music wash over your soul. Close your eyes and allow Vivaldi's "The Four Seasons," Samuel Barber's "Agnus Dei," or Beethoven's "Für Elise" and "Ode to Joy" to reveal a hint of eternity.

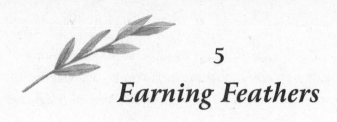

5

Earning Feathers

I can, with one eye squinted, take it all as a blessing.
—FLANNERY O'CONNOR

Draw near to God, and He will draw near to you.
—JAMES 4:8 (NKJV)

How does one live soulfully when the marriage hits a rocky patch, the body hurts, raising kids feels like a pressure cooker, or the health of someone much loved is in dire jeopardy? How about when aging parents demand our attention, the career is thrown a curve ball, or grief has eclipsed our joy?

In other words, how do you live soulfully when you poignantly feel the limits of your humanity?

During my graduate school days in London, my favorite haunt was Holland Park. Early in the morning, I would jog through the serene Kyoto Garden and catch happy glimpses of many a band of squirrels, a Japanese heron, or a sneaking red fox. But the real joy was spying the royal peacocks in all their plumed majesty. Their fans of feathers in iridescent blues and greens, their signature "eye" patterns, and the elegant, otherworldly headdresses make these birds true works of art.

Did you know some say a peacock earns its beautiful feathers by eating thorns? Apparently, the digested spikes contribute to the shape and beauty of their plumage. I am struck by the irony. Maybe its example could apply to our lives as well. Our experiences of pain can present opportunities for transformation.

Judging by some of the pictures posted on Facebook and Instagram, and by our cheerful dispositions in the Sunday pew, you would think life is a rose-petaled path, when the truth is our lives are complex, peppered with setbacks, and near-comically imperfect.

Live long enough and you will know the taste of thorns. The sharp edges of life can cut our spirits from the inside out. Either we throw in the towel or we allow the thorns to transform us into beings more beautiful than ever before. The great Southern author and devout Catholic Flannery O'Connor used the peacock as a literary symbol for resurrection. She believed that the mysterious workings of grace could transform a situation, even a soul. Though she was acquainted with personal tragedy, O'Connor never gave up on God.

So, how do we live soulfully while crunching on thorns?

First, accept this reality: No life is safe from suffering. Though we know this, many of us are still living our lives secretly disappointed, forever shortchanged and bitter. But how might our perspectives shift if we re-imagined obstacles to be the keys that open doors and destinies? Practice patience. Accept the truth imparted in Ecclesiastes 3:1: *There will be a season for everything, a time for every human experience under heaven's rim.* Expect dancing and mourning, tears and laughter, death and opportunities for new life. We will weep for what we thought we needed or deserved only to end up celebrating what we could never have imagined.

Don't lose yourself to a setback. Search your life for blessings daily. Write them down. They are your currency for cashing in on hope. You will be surprised how serendipities appear even in the bleakest of situations. Father Richard Rohr said, "There are no dead ends in this spiritual life. Nothing is above or beyond redemption. Everything can be used for transformation."

Attend to someone who is struggling much more than you. Extend a hand, a pot of chicken soup, or just a prayer. God wisely gave us one another to make our ways through life. When we help another get back up, our own spirits resurrect.

A silver lining to eating "thorns" is a new intimacy with God, which happens in true moments of vulnerability. A holy tête-à-tête with God can move you from fearful shock to faithful strategy. Let the late-night, tear-soaked, white-tiled-bathroom-floor conversations with God change you and your perspective on outcomes. Be confident in the ultimate direction of your life and have the courage to surrender and pray the words "Thy will be done." Watch how God transforms brokenness into blessings, the impossible is made possible, and the thorns become beautiful feathers added to your fan.

Holy One,

The bells peal.
The sun anoints me in dappled light,
forging rays into halos.
Angels gather in the eaves to intone a novena of hope.
Quick, light the lamps within the Cathedral that I am.
You arrive.
(Of course, You are always here and always will be, as
promised.)
I long for a blessing to make my way.

Silence descends.
You process down the nave of my being.
A nod of benediction is mercifully extended to my flaws
tucked sullen in the back pew,
they follow me wherever I go.
Thankfully, You focus on my potential, the good in me.

"Be still," You whisper to my restless soul,
and then climb into the lectern of my heart.
My spirit is suddenly swathed in a glow, supernatural.
A child again.
"I made you for Love,"
You whisper.
"I don't give as the world gives."
The tears come.
"I make a way when you see no way."
"Your soul is unconquerable."

A homily of love—
from the One who knows me
better than I know myself.
I slip back through the iron-filigree doors.
Grace is mine again.
To know this kind of love,
I can do anything.

Humbly, I say Amen.

Tips for Helping Others Through Suffering

WE'VE ALL HAD seasons of "crunching on thorns." Help nourish someone who is suffering, knowing that somewhere along that curving path, we will need someone else to do the same for us. In my own experience raising a child with cancer and fifteen years as a minister of pastoral care, I have collected some meaningful ways to help those in their season of thorns.

1. Show up. Don't worry about what you say; more than likely they won't remember. But they will remember you had the courage to just be there.

2. Send a note, a text, or a postcard in the mail every week for as long as is needed. When my child Charlie was undergoing treatment, a friend who lived six hundred miles away texted me every single day—the same sentence every time: "Just said a prayer for Charlie!" To know that someone stopped in the middle of their day to think of us was a daily reminder that we were not alone.

3. Take a meal that is healthy and nourishing. Loss takes a tremendous toll on one's health in body, mind, and spirit. Tend to their bodies with healthy food, soothing tea and honey, and even include some vitamin C for immunity.

4. Create a hope box. Fill any kind of box with seven individually wrapped gifts. The card simply reads: "Open one each day of the week." Inside each package is a thoughtful gift to lift the spirit. A family friend lost her son tragically, and in her hope box, I included items to create an altar in her house where she could weep, pray, and process the grief. An olive-wood cross, a candle, a prayer cloth,

anointing oils, and a collection of prayers. Choose whatever comes to you as being helpful.

5. Household duties: Clean the kitchen, wash and fold laundry, go to the grocery store, weed the garden, write thank-you notes. Daily chores are especially difficult in the midst of suffering.

6. Instead of sending flowers, consider giving a seedling or potted plant that could be planted in a special place to grow and be a vibrant remembrance. I especially love the Lenten rose that blooms every year during Lent and Easter.

6

Two Stones

The mystery of human existence lies not in just staying alive,
but in finding something to live for.
—FYODOR DOSTOEVSKY

Let us also lay aside every weight, and sin which clings so closely,
and let us run with endurance the race that is set before us.
—HEBREWS 12:1 (ESV)

A spiritual pilgrimage to the Scottish isle of Iona has beckoned and intrigued me for years. The ancient Celts believed this island was a thin place where one could peek through the veil separating the heavens from the earth for a glimpse of the Divine.

Pilgrims to Iona are instructed to choose two stones from the beautiful island's rocky shore.

The first stone represents something he or she must let go of to continue successfully on the life journey. This could be a diminishing relationship, a festering old resentment, or a need for control. In a grand gesture, the pilgrim happily casts this first stone into the sea (or down a hill, or into a green recycle bin, or into the creek behind one's yard!).

The second Iona stone represents something that we desire to take with us. A yearning of long standing. This could be a dream, a career change, a new relationship, a deep hope for the future, or whatever is the heart's desire. Place this second stone in the center of your home (mine sits prominently on my bookshelf). Every time you pass by, you practice awareness of your destiny and open yourself to a new energy.

On trips to visit grandparents in Jackson Hole, I like to jog along the levee beside the Snake River. Scattered along the footpath are these beautiful stone sculptures. One smooth river stone has been placed on top of another until it becomes a holy mound. They are officially called cairns. And for millennia, humans have used them to mark their paths. The stones sanctify some kind of transformation that has taken place. This makes me think of the story of Jacob in the Bible.* As a young man, Jacob goes on a journey of spiritual discovery and picks out a stone to serve as a pillow for a night's rest. In a dream, he has an encounter with the Divine Presence, and it changes his life forever. A promise is made between God and Jacob. Together they will fulfill his holy destiny. Jacob's sleep stone marks the transformation from who he was to all the possibilities of who he could be. Our lives are in a constant state of transformation too. We have to let go to take on.

Find two palm-size rocks of your own and try to use them intentionally through this week to follow the tradition of these two Ionian stones. I challenge you to not play it safe or comfortable. Be open to whatever the cosmos has in store for you, the confounding and the joyous. Pledge to reject mistakes from the past. Adopt a new strategy. The opinions and judgments of family, friends, and colleagues are not necessary or welcome. Seek companionship with God. Welcome transformation, wherever, whenever it comes, that will push you to accomplish a whole life, full of consequence and happiness.

My first stone is control; my second stone is trust. I am going to work

---

* See Genesis 28:11–20.

on relying less on myself and more on God. It's tiring trying to control every vignette of my life, crossing every T and dotting every I perfectly. It's about time I get out of God's way so grace can do its redemptive work. I am going to make more space in my life and heart for God to surprise me. What are yours?

Two stones. A life transformed.

Dear God,

One moment, I am skipping down life's path,
hopeful for where You are leading me.
Next, I am stalled in place,
stonewalled in fear
afraid of the next step.

You chose me for the journey.
Help me to let go of whatever is keeping me
from making my beautiful way.

However my path unfolds,
I know You will see to where I need to be going.
Never alone, never completely lost.
That is Your promise.

Amen.

Meatballs

I am the head chef at a little family restaurant called Bistro Mason. It has one table set with eight chairs, often a couple extra; usually some flowers in a bud vase; and a candle or two. Most nights I plate for eight, with three of my guests being under the age of twelve. The menu is seasonal with a Mediterranean flair. Broccoli, salmon, and blueberries are on regular rotation.

The kitchen table is our secret anchor. Sitting down together for dinner five nights a week is essential to my family. The meal is always blessed, as are the people sitting around the table. This is where we reflect on the highs and lows of our day. It is a safe place to let go of the worry stones that weigh us down: hurt feelings, poor choices, a sackful of what-ifs. In their place, we receive love stones of forgiveness, encouragement, and hope for the following day.

A family favorite at this bistro is my recipe for spaghetti and meatballs. I make them extra healthy by sneaking in the spinach and parsley! You can find my quick recipe for a simple homemade tomato sauce below, or to save time, pick your favorite tomato sauce in a bottle. I like a Nashville brand, Caffe Nonna's Marinara, in a pinch.

Meatball Ingredients

2 large eggs
2 tsp salt
1 tsp dried oregano
freshly ground black pepper
1 cup Parmesan, grated

1½ cups greens—Italian parsley,
    spinach, basil, finely minced
2 lbs ground grass-fed beef
1 cup nonfat plain yogurt
1 cup bread crumbs

Directions

Preheat oven to 400°F. Whisk the eggs in a large bowl until blended. Whisk in your salt, oregano, a generous quantity of black pepper, along with Parmesan and greens. Combine egg mixture with meat, yogurt, and bread crumbs. Use your hands to thoroughly mix the ground meat mixture. Pinch off the mixture a piece at a time and gently roll between your hands to form 1½-inch meatballs. Continue shaping until all the meat is used. Arrange the meatballs spaced slightly apart on a baking sheet. Bake for 25–30 minutes. The meatballs are done when cooked through and the outsides are browned, or when they register 165°F in the middle on an instant-read thermometer.

Tomato Sauce Ingredients

4 containers cherry tomatoes
    (variety is nice!)
olive oil
1 tbsp herbes de Provence
½ tsp kosher salt
fresh-ground pepper

½ cup Parmesan, grated, more
    for garnish
½ cup fresh basil, chopped
1 tsp dried oregano
1 tbsp brown sugar

Directions

Preheat oven to 400°F. On a baking sheet covered in parchment or foil, arrange your cherry tomatoes. Generously bathe them in olive oil, then sprinkle over top the herbes de Provence, kosher salt, and fresh-ground pepper. Bake until they are bubbly (10–15 minutes). Pour the entire tray, juices and all, into a blender. Add Parmesan, basil, oregano, and sugar, then blend well. Add salt and pepper (and more sugar, if too acidic) to taste.

Heat sauce (homemade or store-bought) in a sauté pan and add meatballs. Serve over a mound of spaghetti with a generous dusting of grated Parmesan. Accompany with a simple arugula salad topped with Parmesan ribbons and dressed with olive oil, juice from 1 lemon, and kosher salt. For my kids, I roast broccolini and dress with lemon juice and grated Parmesan.

7

Your Life Is Your Prayer

The day of my spiritual awakening was the day I saw—and knew
I saw—all things in God and God in all things.
—MECHTHILD OF MAGDEBURG

Therefore I tell you, whatever you ask for in prayer, believe that
you have received it, and it will be yours.
—MARK 11:24 (NIV)

On a summer trip to Jackson Hole, I conquered a personal fear. The
trip was jam-packed with activities. We hiked, fished, floated the
Snake River, rode horses, roasted marshmallows, and took the tram to
the top of the ski mountain for waffles. We even survived an invasion of
bats and the ensuing all-family rabies vaccinations. It was a blast, truly
(even the unsavory bat incident), until our trip to the Aerial Ropes Course.

I was meant to be the family photographer on this outing. Everyone
knows Mom isn't a fan of heights. I panicked when the outfitter said both
parents would need to be eighty feet in the air to chaperone our four kids.
This particular ropes course is billed as "challenging" and requires a
twenty-minute training session to even get the green light to make the
climb up!

Three different courses were offered: beginner, intermediate, and advanced. All was going surprisingly well as I was following my then seven-
year-old daughter Rose up the intermediate course, moving through the
log crossing, the acrobatic wire, and the spider web, until we finally

reached the top platform. I had completed the course without a hitch! It never crossed my mind to ask how we would get down. Before I knew it, a college-age kid was hooking me into a silver line and instructing me to carefully step up to the pair of black-sticker footprints at the edge of the platform, eighty feet up. "Excuse me? I'm not going off this. I'll trace my steps back." With a chuckle, he said, "It's the only way, lady. You have to step off the platform. Everyone has to take the leap."

It was becoming embarrassing how long I stood frozen on those two footprints. Finally, with some husbandly encouragement from the safe ground below, I stepped out into the air, hollering for all the Tetons to hear me. To my great surprise, the rope caught my free fall, and I glided gracefully the remaining fifty feet down to safety.

Authentic prayer requires a leap. There is no other way.

To close your eyes, open your heart, and trust your vulnerable self to something unseen, infinite, and vast definitely requires a leap of faith. And yet, it is the secret to being tucked safely under the wings of God while still roped into the harness of our flesh and bone. Regular prayer is the only way I have a chance to find peace with six kids, four dogs, four beehives, sometimes a fish, and a husband in this topsy-turvy world.

Prayer is a miraculous yet sometimes frustrating effort. Not only is the receiver unseen, but we never really know if our pleadings are heard or when they will be answered. I am a novitiate in the art of praying. Sometimes my prayers feel surface-deep—sometimes laboriously rote. I try to pray with conviction, but often my words are clumsy, inelegant, or self-conscious. But I will not stop reaching for God.

Vulnerability and speaking our raw truths are the first lessons on how to pray. After all, prayer is the language of our souls. Even still, the practice of prayer is lifelong and evolving. Some nights, I simply and quietly kneel beside my bed at the close of a challenging day. During my son's cancer treatment, I daily lit a candle in the chapel next to the hospital. When I struggle for words, the Psalms become my prayers. Silence in the woods becomes a tender prayer. I tearfully cry out to heaven, "Help me!" Some days I forget to pray, and then on others, I find myself whispering prayers with every breath. The prayer I whisper the most is: "Dear God, Where am I? Where are you? Please close the distance."

Formal, polite prayers are insufficient and fool no one, especially God. A sincere and open heart is the surest way to get God's attention. What I can tell you in my experience with prayer is that God meets us where we are. And there is never judgment or crazy expectations with God. Most of us are doing our very best to find our way with a measure of grace, and God knows it.

There is no perfect prayer or pray-er. I used to feel guilty about the lack of discipline in my prayer life until I expanded what prayer is for me. What if, actually, the way I live my life could be a prayer? What if lighting a candle in a chapel, cooking a meal for a friend in need, enjoying a belly laugh with my six-year-old, doing yoga in the yard, singing a poor rendition of "Amazing Grace" at bedtime to my son, are all prayers? Suddenly, my daily life becomes a sacred liturgy, the ordinary ministrations become living prayers. Life is experienced as a little more sacred.

Be inspired by all the creative ways you can invite God into the rolling conversation of your life.

Creator of me,

When I close my eyes,
slow my breath,
and ask You to enter in—

I feel the shift in gravity.
You are here.
No longer am I relying on myself
and the material world for my grounding and truth.
Just You—the One whose Love never fails.

Help me rediscover the place of holiness inside me.
That part of me drawn to hope,
refusing to give in to despair,
seeing first the goodness in others,
and viewing Your world
with a sense of wonder and awe.

Grace after grace you show me.
Help me to see that in every breath something
sacred is at stake.
With courage, I will walk forward,
knowing without knowing,
toward You, with You,
and for You.

A holiest Amen.

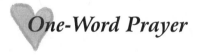

One-Word Prayer

A FEW YEARS ago I was invited to a retreat on centering prayer at St. Mary's Convent in Sewanee, Tennessee. It could not have come at a better time for me. I had just come through two years of cancer treatment for my son and welcomed a new baby. Overwhelmed inside and out was my state of mind. I was trying my best to cross my T's and dot my I's as a mother and wife, but with very little tranquility, unmoored from myself and my God. At St. Mary's, I practiced centering prayer and found again my calm center. I appreciate the simplicity of the one-word prayer, especially when I feel like a spinning top.

Try this introductory practice to centering prayer.

1. Take a comfortable seated position. Lay your palms faceup on your thighs. Close your eyes. Direct your mind to silence. Relinquish expectations, self-doubt, and that laundry list of to-dos and worries.

2. Choose a particular word or phrase that soothes or reflects your secret longing in the present moment. Words that I use are *hope, be still, beloved, calm,* and *peace.*

3. Repeat your sacred "code word" in between slow, measured inhales and exhales. Expect that other unwanted thoughts will enter your mind and distract you. Imagine these interruptions as weather and just let them pass by. Keep returning to your centering word. Focusing on the word allows your mind and body to relax so you can slip into an envelope of peace.

4. Close your session with this affirmation: "I am loved. I am enough."

8

"No Mud, No Lotus"

Because you are alive, everything is possible.
—THICH NHAT HANH

But those who wait for the Lord shall renew their strength;
they shall mount up with wings like eagles; they shall run and not
be weary; they shall walk and not faint.
—ISAIAH 40:31 (ESV)

It was a serendipitous gift to attend the premiere of Thich Nhat Hanh's calligraphy exhibit in New York City, with over eighty original works of art by the renowned Buddhist monk. They are a wondrous result of his private meditative practices. Imagine crisp white linen sheets of paper watermarked in black ink with words of profound wisdom. Thich Nhat Hanh's artistic process starts with him preparing a cup of black tea, then adding a drop of this elixir to his calligraphy ink. In thoughtful meditation, he then puts pen to paper. Some of his inspired messages titling the art pieces are "Breathe, you are alive," "I have arrived, I am home," and "Go as a river." One that especially caught my eye was "No mud, no lotus."

The lovely lotus blooms out of disagreeable mud. Thich Nhat Hanh uses this natural phenomenon as a metaphor for our own happiness that does not exist apart from our suffering. The beauty of the lotus is in its determination to rise out of the darkness to meet the sun, transformed.

Adversity is inherent to our human condition. We do everything in our power to run from, protect against, and numb the uncomfortable and painful parts of being human. Yet it's the mud that defines us—illuminates us.

The most interesting and often profound examples of humanity at its best are when the spirit rises hand over fist out of the muck to become something more worthy (exquisite, even) than before.

In the biblical story of Jonah and the whale, the prophet tries his best to hide from suffering, and yet he still ends up in the terrifying sea beast's belly. Is there anyone who hasn't spent some time in the mud or the dark gut of a sea beast? I don't care how intelligent, lucky, or superhuman you think you are. You are still only flesh and bone. And if you have lived on this planet long enough or dared to invest your heart in someone or something other than yourself, you've experienced the prick of suffering.

But remember, the elegant lotus blooms out of the mire, and the burning phoenix rises from its own ashes; likewise it is promised for humans that resurrection will follow death. Light will breach the darkness. As the author and psychiatrist Elisabeth Kübler-Ross said, "Beautiful people do not just happen."

The divine story of Creator and creation is a love narrative brimming with vignettes where the protagonists (that would be you and me) are repeatedly knocked down in the mud only to rise up redeemed. It is in the dark and challenging moments of our lives where we either fold or discover our wings.

The next time you find yourself soulflat in the mud, try to shift your perspective from obstacle to opportunity. Something from the experience will strengthen you. You will discover an inner courage and an expansiveness of your faith in "the pits." This is rich ground for finding "our people"—those who truly love us and willingly enter the dark and messy to help us resurrect. Lean into God for reinforcement. Remember, God created both lotus and human spirit to rise and meet the sun.

Dear God,

I am on a mission
to leave this
world with a
larger-than-life spirit.
Strong, resilient,
passionate, and daring,
till my last breath.
I want the full-spectrum experience:
Joys, triumphs, silver linings.
A real showing of spiritual gusto.
Never to meet a stranger.
Be a fool for love,
always reaching out heart-in-hand to the world.
A constellation of hope that will not burn out.
A lotus rising to meet the sun.
Your doppelgänger.
This is my prayer, oh God.

Amen.

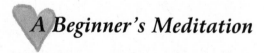

A Beginner's Meditation

SOULFULL RESILIENCE BEGINS with being centered. When we are sure of who we are at our core and confident that God is moving us in an ultimate direction of redemption, we can access an inner strength and peace to meet the struggle. One way to build our resilience muscles is through meditation. I have chosen Psalm 46:10 to guide our meditation. Take a comfortable seated position in a quiet space, absent your phone. Make sure you have allowed yourself a buffer of seven minutes to disengage. Close your eyes. Take in three deep, measured breaths through your nose, and exhale energetically through your mouth. Next take a deep breath in through your nose, let it out through your nose, and then see how long you can calmly wait before taking another calm breath. Repeat three more times, calmly lengthening the seconds between the breaths. It is in the momentary "not breathing" that you signal to your mind, body, and soul that it is okay to flip the inner switch and welcome peace.

The initial breathing exercise prepares us for the meditation below:

As you breathe in, allow your spirit to silently say: "Be still."
As you exhale, say: "And know."
(Repeat three times, with two-count breath measure.)
Next, as you breathe in, say: "Be still and know."
As you exhale, say: "I am God."
(Repeat three times, with three-count breath measure.)
Now sit peacefully in this timeless, safe space of inner quiet. Every time your mind begins to latch on to a thought, return to the mantra: "Be still. And know."

To close the meditation, say aloud: "Thank you, God, for allowing me to slip into Your space and breathe Your air. These moments of inner quiet will sustain me today. Until we meet again."

9

The Secret Life of Bees

In the name of the Bee—
And of the Butterfly—
And of the Breeze—Amen!
—EMILY DICKINSON

For in him we live and move and have our being.
—ACTS 17:28 (NIV)

I am an eager novice beekeeper. My first season led me to believe I was a natural. All three of my hives produced gallons of honey. I gifted family, friends, and strangers with the sweet golden elixir. My second season was during the pandemic. The Bee Universe was determined to humble me on all fronts.

Two of my queens either abandoned ship or died before the spring pollen season, leaving me in such despair. I rush-ordered two queen bees from Hawaii. These ladies arrived in Tennessee accompanied by their courts of worker bees. I visited the hives most days with conversation, music, and sugar water. Despite my best efforts, the production was much smaller the second year. The third year was a catastrophe. I lost all the hives and sadly returned to buying honey from the local grocery store.

Beekeeping is a master class in patience, humor, and perseverance. Every season, I navigate a roller-coaster ride of stinging (literally) losses with some sweet rewards. I have made record mistakes in my short tenure as a beekeeper. My husband loves to tell the story of an early spring evening when he heard my squeals and watched me through the kitchen window, stripping off my clothes down to my "birthday suit" in the front yard as an angry swarm of bees chased me into the house. I had welts up and down my legs and arms for days!

I became a beekeeper for three reasons: One, I love honey. Could there be anything better than a cup of tea with a swirl of honey, or a baguette sliced, toasted, and smeared with butter and honey? Two, I know that bees are integral to the health and survival of our planet. And three, having watched a friend working in his hive, a portrait of calm in the center of a bee-swarm storm, I wanted to attain his capacity for peace in the face of my chaotic hive of a life.

Could becoming a beekeeper coax out a better version of myself?

I admire my bees because although their lives are short, they are filled with great purpose and membership in a cohesive, even loving, community. There is a special harmony in a bee's life that I long for in my own. Although, it is unnerving when the hive is open and I am surrounded on all sides by a swarm of bees with their ready stingers. Any beekeeper will tell you that no matter how well you are protected or how extensive your expertise, you can still get stung. This tension is the same in our everyday lives. At any given moment, we can be surprised by something good or bad, like a diagnosis or the loss of someone or something important to us. None of us can avoid the visible and invisible welts that come with being human in a broken world. Too often we see through an aperture of fear and try to control every possible circumstance, so as not to be disappointed or painfully stung. The result is a very small life and much less joy. What would change inside our souls if we chose to mirror the seasoned beekeeper's posture of trust, surrender, and peace?

The first couple of years, I was afraid every single time I opened the hives' boxes. I remember the shock of the first sting. I wanted to run, cry, even toss my beekeeping suit in the garbage. "I've been stung." Do you know my bee mentor's response? "Yep. It happens. Carry on."

The best advice in beekeeping and life is to not panic in a swarm. An important spiritual discipline is learning how to cultivate inner calm in the tension. When all my hives are open and I am covered head to toe in bees, the sound of their angry buzzing in my ears, my first instinct is to panic and run. I am practicing how to be less reactive, more steady. To be a nonanxious presence around the hives and in my daily life. I close my eyes, slow my movements, and just breathe. Miraculous how the bees (and humans alike) respond. Eventually they return to work, and I am free to continue.

I am happy to report my fourth year was a "sweet" success. My four new hives produced several gallons of honey. More importantly, I am learning how to bring a calmer, gentler version of myself to the hives and to my family, friends, and work.

Holy and Loving God,

I come to You because You loved me first.
I come with questions the world cannot answer.
I come to lay before You
my disappointments, my doubts, my dreams,
my soul longings.
I come for mercy because in some conversation
I allowed my ego to speak over my soul.
I come because I don't want to be afraid anymore.
And You are the only One
who can smooth my edges serene.

I come to feel something exquisite,
not of this world,
but of heaven.
I come because suddenly things become possible
when You are involved.
I come to say thank you for the whole of it.
I come because why would I not come?
You are the source of all that is good and miraculous,
hopeful and redemptive.
And, You love me.

Amen.

Sweet Nectarine, Pistachio, Basil, and Honey Mozza Salad

Beekeepers look forward to the honey harvest all year long. Early in my beekeeping, I was taken under the wing of a seasoned bee-keeper. He has become a generous friend and mentor. Every August, we gather for a daylong honey harvest extravaganza. I host a celebration dinner in the evening. Honey is the star ingredient in every single dish. A favorite is my mozzarella salad with cherry to-matoes, ripe and juicy nectarines, creamy buffalo mozzarella, fresh basil, roasted pistachios, buttery olive oil, and aged balsamic, with the pièce de résistance—a generous swirl of honey. You can hap-pily substitute the nectarines for peaches, cherries, or strawberries in season.

Ingredients

1 bushel cherry tomatoes,
    a medley of colors, split in half
handful of fresh basil
1 container of buffalo mozzarella
2 ripe nectarines, sliced with
    skin on

½ cup roasted pistachio nuts
½ cup high-quality olive oil
2 tbsp balsamic vinegar
2 tbsp honey (lavender or rosemary
    honey would be a treat)
salt and pepper

Directions

Arrange tomatoes, nectarines, and mozzarella on a plate. Decorate with whole basil leaves or a chiffonade of leaves, and sprinkle pistachios. Drizzle with olive oil, balsamic vinegar, warmed honey, salt, and pepper! Enjoy the easiest, most beautiful, and happiest recipe in the book!

10

It's a da Vinci

If you only look at us, you might well miss the brightness.
We carry this precious Message around in the
unadorned clay pots of our ordinary lives.
—EUGENE PETERSON*

You are the light of the world—like a city on a hilltop
that cannot be hidden.
—MATTHEW 5:14 (NLT)

For over forty years, Basil Clovis Hendry, Sr., was the director of the men's choir for Our Lady of Mercy Catholic Church in Baton Rouge, Louisiana. If you visited his home, you might have noticed an oil painting of Jesus dressed in a rich azure robe, with his right hand raised in benediction, his left hand grasping an orb. For over five decades, Mr. Hendry and his family were in possession of a treasure of incredible value, a work by none other than the magnificent Renaissance master Leonardo da Vinci. And they never knew it!

Mr. Hendry inherited the masterpiece from his aunt Minnie, an art and antiques dealer, who purchased it for a steal in 1958. Over the course of the last five hundred years, the "Salvator Mundi" masterpiece had graced the walls of Italian princes, French kings, Russian oligarchs, and a humble Southern choir director in Louisiana. Recently, the da Vinci sold for a

---

* See also 2 Corinthians 4:7, MSG

whopping $450 million to the crown prince of Saudi Arabia, making it one of the most valuable paintings of all time.

Hendry's daughter, a retired librarian, told *The Wall Street Journal*, "We can't believe it, that such an incredible piece could have been in our family, and we didn't even know it all this time."

What if I told you that you have in your own possession a treasure of remarkable value? For however many years you have been alive, the metaphorical da Vinci has been in your possession. Your soul is a masterpiece of creation.

The soul is the most noble part of our being. It is the command center at our heart, inwardly in touch with God, outwardly seeking goodness, meaning, and purpose.

In 2 Corinthians 4:7–12, Paul compares the soul hidden in the human frame to a treasure kept in a clay jar. The metaphor would have easily resonated with his first-century audience, as they stored their most valuable olive oils and wines in terra-cotta amphorae. He urgently wanted the community in Corinth to know that their lives were sacred, with holy purpose. You and I have the same capacity to love and act in the world as God's glorious proxies. We are made of earth but also of heaven. No matter how fragile our "earthly" containers or the challenges life presents, ultimately our value is as a carrier of the Divine spark. We are living "glory jars."

The divinity within us is of infinite value, waiting to be discovered and then shared with the world. We will not find the treasure by having, doing, and being more. That is the ego's agenda. Sometimes we must learn the hard way that what the world deems "treasure"—professional success and material possessions, health and beauty, comfort and security—has a shine but never lasts. The soul offers more. It whispers, *I am of God.*

I recently rediscovered the special book *A Book of Hours* by Thomas

Merton. Merton wrote, "We do not know we are full of paradise because we are so full of our own noise that we cannot hear God singing us and all things into being." I am learning that when I am harried, self-focused, and feeling a little lackluster, the world does not receive the best from me.

Are we listening to our souls? Do we acknowledge this divinity in ourselves and others? Or are we so caught up with what the clay pot looks like on the outside and the world's expectations of us that we forget the everlasting glory inside?

The soulfull life begins the moment we acknowledge that we are more than dust—so much more—and choose to live from and for our souls. It is our only chance of seeing and experiencing the world through the eyes of God.

Beloved,

Humbly I stand before You,
more than a collection of pottery dust,
I am a carrier of the Divine spark,
with a sacred mission.
"Live from my soul," You say.
The reward, of course, is a holy adventure.
May I never lose heart.
Outwardly, I may appear fragile.
Inwardly, You are renewing me every single day.
No matter how this Life chips away at the clay,
I will persevere.
Suffer and rise.
Love to my fullest capacity.

Live hope to hope.
May I never forget the "glory" in the jar.

A most grateful Amen.

Lavender and Roman Chamomile
Essential Healing Oils

And thou shalt sanctify them [with oil], that they may be most holy.
—EXODUS 30:29 (KJV)

The spiritual practice of anointing with fragrant oils has always intrigued me. In the Bible, anointing the body and head with oil
marked a person or event as holy. In the Letter to the Hebrews,
God is described anointing Jesus with the "oil of gladness." Early
Christians anointed guests entering their homes with perfumed
oils as an act of hospitality. Pilgrims would anoint themselves
and their footpaths to the Holy Land. Ancient recipes for
healing oils using cinnamon, myrrh, and frankincense can
be found in the Bible. Anointing the sick and dying is one
of the holy sacraments of the Christian church. The pure
olfactory impact of lavender, rosemary, rose, or Roman
chamomile can positively affect mind, body, and spirit,
even transport us to another plane of peace.

Aromatherapy oils have been scientifically proven
to elevate mood, boost the immune system, and improve emotional and physical well-being. Smelling

peppermint, rosemary, and eucalyptus can ease a migraine head-ache. For centuries, lavender has encouraged relaxation and sleep. This week, try putting lavender essential oil on the bottoms of your feet, just below your nose, and behind your ears before bed to cultivate calm and a renewed lightness of being.

Several years ago, I started blending my own healing oils. Using jojoba or coconut oil as my base, I mix in drops of lavender, Roman chamomile, bergamot, and frankincense to create a balm of tranquility–also a lovely perfume. Rub the oil into pressure points, massage into muscles, dot on the wrists and behind the ears, or enjoy in a heavenly bath.

Ingredients

8 drops lavender oil

6 drops Roman chamomile oil

3 drops bergamot oil

2 drops frankincense oil

10 ml jojoba oil

Directions

Fill a small glass bottle or rollerball with your jojoba oil followed by your drops of lavender, Roman chamomile, frankincense, and bergamot. Be inspired to play around with the scents to create your own blend.

11

Roll with It

Heaven is now and forever for those
who are willing to keep changing.
—ROBERT P. VANDE KAPPELLE

There is a time for everything, and a season
for every activity under the heavens.
—ECCLESIASTES 3:1 (NIV)

A decade ago, I happily sat at a lively dinner table while on a family beach vacation with my parents, my husband, and my then three children. All these loved ones surrounded me as I blew out my thirty-three birthday candles and made a heartfelt wish. Sun-kissed by life, I wished for things to stay exactly as they were in that very happy moment. How naive and limiting a prayer! Over the next decade, I welcomed three more children. I built a special nest with my soulmate and started a new job uncovering the tiny diamond-in-the-rough of me. New Zealand was crossed off our family bucket list, a trip of a lifetime. I wrote *The Pocket Cathedral*, a book of prayers for fellow travelers seeking a way to God. In the same decade, I lost precious people I loved, broke my shoulder and two ankles, suffered a miscarriage, was denied a book deal, endured the fracture of a close relationship, and sold that forever nest. In my wildest dreams, I could not have imagined such a roller-coaster ride!

Euripides wrote, "Nothing is secure, nothing keeps." What a "rip the Band-Aid off" truth about the human condition! Nothing ever stays the same. Not your honeymoon marriage, not your oldest friendships, not your innocent perspective, not glorious nature, not your youthful appearance, not your prayers, or even your view of God. This is by divine design. From the moment the first atom split, God has been pushing the creative envelope: expanding, improving, evolving creation. The Creator is not interested in what once was but only in what could and ultimately will be.

Do you struggle with change? It is my spiritual Achilles' heel. I have built more walls than windmills in the face of life's changing circumstances. I fear the unknown. I know I'm not alone in this admission. The slightest shift in the compass of life can cause the steeliest sailor to lose his sea legs, the most devout disciple to question whether the Holy Center will hold. But change is exactly how God moves your story and mine forward.

The "holy project" that is our life would be a failure if we are the same people when we leave this world as we were when we started. Always we are in a process of letting go of something to make room for a new reality. We grieve because it is difficult to forgo the safe, comfortable, and known for the new and unknown. We angst, backpedal, hurt, even curse God, begging for things to return to the way they were. Time spent in the strange land between what once was and what will be is a spiritual purgatory. These are soul-searching and stretching times, a true remapping of reality. But God does not allow us to stagnate. God's love keeps us moving forward. Have faith—and remember: The unknown is known to God.

The most successful human beings accept and then adapt to changing circumstances. And they do it again and again. God programmed us to evolve. Don't panic. Be patient. There is always a path forward, God promises it. Instead of avoiding, fighting, or running from change, mine the experience for clues as to what God wants you to see, do, and accomplish next. Beware of the ego. It gets in the way of enjoying the ride and slows our spiritual becoming. The ego fears what it cannot control. This can cause such a lot of misery. The soul, on the other hand, knows there is no real end, nothing is wasted, and everything will ultimately come together for good on the canvas of life.

"Forget the former things; do not dwell on the past. See, I am doing a new thing! Now it springs up; do you not perceive it? I am making a way in the wilderness and streams in the wasteland."* This is God's promise. Spend less time worrying about what has happened in the past or what could go wrong in the future and more time anticipating what will go right. One way to navigate change is to hold the present and future loosely. Fear has us trying to control every breath. There is freedom in surrendering to God's plan for our lives. Be curious and open to what God has next up the Divine sleeve. Make room for grace to do something new in your life. This is called living in hope.

Dear God,

Produce in me a measure of hope
to keep stepping forward.
Produce in me some inner clarity
in all life's contradictions.
Produce in me a truth
that will stand firm in the face of all the untruths.
Produce in me a sword
to slay my ego, so I can finally be the noble me.
Produce in me a fertile field

---

* Isaiah 43:19, NIV

to sow mercy upon mercy.
Produce in me a love that saves.

Amen.

Southern Fruit Cobbler

In the whirl of change, we look to traditions, rituals, people, music, places, and even recipes to comfort and ground us. This family recipe for a healthy, gluten-free, and delicious fruit crisp (or, as Southerners like to call it, fruit cobbler) returns you metaphorically home, to a place of warmth, sweetness, and joy.

Ingredients

1 cup oat flour
½ cup almond meal
1½ cups turbinado sugar
1 tsp baking powder
½ tsp kosher salt
1½ cups oats

1 tsp vanilla
4 cups peaches, peeled and sliced.
　　(In season, I love to substitute
　　blackberries for peaches, and
　　use apples with cinnamon in
　　the winter)

½ stick–1 stick butter (I use the
   salted Kerrygold Irish butter),
   cut into bite-size chunks

orange blossom water (optional)
¼ cup sugar (optional)
zest of orange or lemon (optional)

Directions

Preheat oven to 400°F. Combine dry ingredients in one bowl with vanilla and set aside. In a separate bowl, combine the fruit with ¼ cup of sugar if the fruit is not sweet, as well as the zest of an orange or lemon, or a splash of orange blossom water for fragrance. Cover bottom of a 9x13" baking dish with fruit mixture. Cover fruit with dry mixture. I use half the dry ingredients for the first cobbler and then save the remaining in a Ziploc bag in the refrigerator for a later use. Decorate top evenly with bite-size pats of butter. Bake in oven for 1 hour. Serve with vanilla bean gelato!

12

Lighten Your Pack

Joy is knowing, even for a moment, that underneath
everything are the everlasting arms.
—FREDERICK BUECHNER

He restores my soul.
—PSALM 23:3 (NRSV)

Scott Guenther is my husband's cousin, but more famously—as a lead ranger at Grand Teton National Park in Jackson, Wyoming—he is a living legend and a beloved local hero. People in trouble meet Scott hanging from a helicopter at ten thousand feet when he comes to rescue them off a treacherous peak.

One night over dinner he shared one of his most harrowing rescues. A massive storm had come up quickly over the Grand Teton. Several climbers were struck by lightning and gravely burned, and some were still barely clinging to the face of the mountain. The weather conditions were unsafe to fly, so Scott made the executive decision for his team to rescue the stranded climbers on foot. Normally, reaching the peak of the Grand Teton takes advanced hikers five-plus hours. Scott did it in half the time and saved several lives that day.

When I asked him his secret, he smiled and said, "I travel with a light pack."

In the synoptic gospels, Jesus gives his disciples some "travel advice" too. "Take no gold, or silver, or copper in your belts, no bag for your journey, or two tunics, or sandals, or a staff."* On the journey with Jesus, he was talking about not only physical baggage but all the invisible burdens we carry around that are weighing us down. God beckons us to lighten our internal load.

I easily pack light for trips, but in everyday life, I lug around an invisible backpack of unresolved hurts and fears. They rob me of joy and slow my spirit's gait. One night I read to the kids from Charlie Mackesy's beautiful book, *The Boy, the Mole, the Fox, and the Horse,* and I came across this truism: "'Isn't it odd. We can only see our outsides, but nearly everything happens on the inside,' said the Mole to the Boy."

Jesus knew the burdens of every human. He lived them on Earth too. In his miracles, he addresses the pains of the human heart first, then heals the external. The mission was to set people free to live abundantly and inspire them to do the same for others.

The more we participate in this brutal and beautiful world, the greater the accumulation of weight in our interior backpacks. The spiritual work is deciphering what is healthy and what we must discard to reach our next peak. We are not mythic Atlases, cursed to carry the whole world on our shoulders. Jesus offers to carry some of the weight.

A wonderfully funny friend of my mom's once told me that she had turned over the same worry to God sixty times. The problem was she had taken it right back fifty-nine of those times. Lightening the soul requires self-awareness and effort. The angst may be passed back and forth from your hands to God's an infinite number of times before you finally release it and embrace God's peace in its place.

The spiritual work for those first disciples and for us today is the same. To figure a way, like Ranger Scott did, to travel with a light pack. This

* Matthew 10:9–10, NRSV

week, I challenge you to pick one worry, fear, or hurt. Pray to God that this weight on your shoulders will loosen its hold on you, and then practice meditatively letting it go. Do this as many times as you need, even if it's fifty-nine times. On the sixtieth, you might finally feel the weight lift from your soul so joy can take its place. The mission is to move with lightness—always forward.

Beloved,

If I could ask of You one thing,
what would it be?
To see into the future?
To stop the worrying?
A glimpse at Your Master Plan?
Answers would be nice,
to life's impossible questions.
Could I have Your word that one day all will be well?

I really would like to ask about the Hereafter.
Does something marvelous await my spirit?
Maybe I'll ask how to love like You love,
forgive like You forgive.
I could certainly ask for more joy
and a little of that peace beyond all understanding.
Or shall I just say thank you?

But what I really want to ask:
Will You be with me?

This is my prayer: Be with me.
Now. Whatever happens. Forever.

Amen.

Yoga Flow

FIFTEEN YEARS AGO, I signed up for a yoga class with my teacher, Adi—now mentor and friend—who guided me through my first vinyasa flow. Yoga is an ancient meditation method that focuses on letting go of the weight and tension of the earthly world so the spirit can enjoy a lightness of being. A "flow" in yoga is a series of postures guided by the breath. Yoga has given me a new appreciation for my body and its capacity for strength, balance, and inner peace. It is my secret weapon for cultivating inner calm and a good night's sleep. I flow through a series of poses every night before bed to calm my mind, relieve stress, and stretch my body. The instant my feet step up to the front of my mat and my hands form in a prayer posture at my heart, I am drawn into a calmer state of being, and the tensions of the day begin to melt away. For me, yoga is a physical expression of prayer. Following is an introductory sequence of poses for a classic Sun Salutation moving meditation.

1. Bring your feet together or hip-width apart at the front of your mat. Place your palms together at the front of your heart and begin to breathe slow, smooth, full breaths through your nose. Adi taught me to use the joined thumbs in prayer pose to lift my heart a little higher. Take a moment to silently set an intention for your practice. I aim for a softness in body, mind, and spirit.

2. Guided by a deep inhale, raise your arms out and up to the sky, palms connected in a prayer pose above your head. Gaze up at your hands. Pause and take a slow, measured inhale and exhale.

3. Release your arms and swan dive over your legs, releasing your hands to your shins or the floor. Relax your head and neck, and gaze softly toward your nose.

4. Guided by an inhale, lift your head, with hands resting on your shins, create a flat back, and gaze forward.

5. Bend your knees, place your hands on the floor, and step back into a plank pose. Your shoulders are aligned over your wrists, hands rooted to the ground, and your lower body is lifted and strong. A good test is if someone could safely place a cup of tea on your stable, flat back. Charge up strength in your arms and core.

6. Now lower your whole body to the mat, hands tucked under your shoulders, point your toes, and lift your chest toward the sun, rolling your shoulders back into a gentle back bend. Look up. Take one slow, measured inhale and exhale.

8. Next press your hips up and back into the famous downward-facing dog pose. Your body should be in a V shape. Close your eyes and rest here for two inhales and exhales. I will often do downward-facing dog as a stand-alone pose because it is an all-body stretch that feels so good.

9. Step right foot and then left to the front of your mat. Lift your arms like wings to the sun, gaze up toward your thumbs, and then release your hands into prayer posture at your heart.

10. Move consciously through this "flow" three to five times. In preparation for a good night's sleep, I finish with a resting pose. Lie on

your back with your arms comfortably at your side, palms facing up; tuck your shoulder blades under you for support; separate your legs; and allow them to fall comfortably open to the sides. Allow your body to melt into the floor. Rest here for as long as you need to feel completely relaxed. I have been known to drift off to sleep in this pose! To come out, fold over to your left or right into a fetal position, and then use your arms to push yourself up to sitting, and then standing.

Sweet dreams!

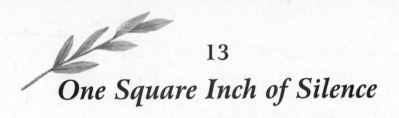

13

One Square Inch of Silence

I am always learning the same thing: there is no other way to live
than this, still, and grateful, and full of longing.
—Eric Gamalinda

I long to dwell in your tent forever and take refuge in
the shelter of your wings.
—Psalm 61:4 (NIV)

One Square Inch of Silence is a geographic location in the Hoh Rain
Forest of Olympic National Park and has been named the quietest
place in the United States. A friend of mine made a pilgrimage to this
unique spot, and she was convinced that she had stepped through the veil
and experienced something of heaven. I hope to visit someday. Gordon
Hempton, the discoverer, is an acoustic ecologist who travels the globe
tracking the few remaining quiet places on Earth. He has recorded the
unique acoustics inside volcanos, the musical scores of rain forests, and
the soundscapes of sunrises across every continent. What Hempton has
concluded, and what is somewhat alarming for humanity, is how few
quiet places remain on our planet, untainted by the noise of modern life.
He believes that we are living in the age of the extinction of silence.

From a quiet monastery to my own bustling reality, I am rediscovering
and cultivating one square inch of silence within myself. Some days better
than others.

I was invited and spiritually led to the Abbey of Our Lady of Gethsemani, a Cistercian monastery of silence tucked in the rolling emerald hills of Kentucky. Imagine a sleepover with fifty monks, where you pray seven times a day, silence is the house rule, and there is no contact with the outside world. What an adventure!*

The monks of Gethsemani give up worldly living to devote their lives to prayer and the study and contemplation of God within their hidden community. A couple of times a year, they allow women to come and participate in the monastic life. I had no idea what I was getting myself into.

First, I was not prepared for the silence policy! There were signs all over the monastery that read, SILENCE IS THE ONLY LANGUAGE SPOKEN HERE! Imagine not speaking a single word for three days! There was no internet, no iPhone, no computer. Even my meals were taken in total silence. The first day was treacherous. After a couple of hours, I literally hiked up a mountain with my cell phone to call home. By the second day, I had somewhat settled into the quiet and was surprised how content I became to just be with myself.

Silence scares us. The discomfort explains why we dearly hold on to our iPhones and have the TV blaring twenty-four hours a day. We feel strangely protected hiding in the world's racket. And yet, what are we not hearing? The monks believe silence is the true path to understanding who we are, who God is, and what our destiny is on this planet.

The brothers of Gethsemani participate in the Liturgy of the Hours, which means they pray seven times a day.† A monk's day begins at 3:15 A.M. with Vigil and ends after the 7:30 P.M. Compline service. I must confess I slept through the 3:15 A.M. service, arrived at the 5:45 A.M. ser-

---

* The monastery was home to one of my favorite authors, the Trappist monk Thomas Merton.
† 3:15 A.M. Vigil, 5:45 A.M. Lauds, 7:30 A.M. Terce, 12:15 P.M. Sext, 2:15 P.M. Nones, 5:30 P.M. Vespers, 7:30 P.M. Compline

vice in my PJs, and then was up and rolling by the 7:30 A.M. prayer. Just when I sat down to write, the bells would peal, marking prayer time, and I would sprint back to the chapel for yet another service.

Talk about God interrupting your life! And yet this was a powerful experience for me. In every service sung by the monks, old, familiar scripture sounded more beautiful than I had experienced before. My favorite time was Compline. The brothers believe this service is the most important: "We gather in the night, in the awareness of the dark forces within us, turn toward the light, confident in the coming of the dawn." I felt the monks were singing a lullaby to my soul.

We all inhabit a very loud, too busy, and often negative exterior landscape. We must learn to "cultivate calm" and engage the world more from a posture of peace. Yet very few of us can do it. The absence of quiet and stillness in our lives has led to the creation of impatient and less hopeful versions of ourselves.

One square inch of silence was a priority for Jesus. His first-century life was noisy, demanding, and full of uncertainty, fear, and violence. Fully embracing our human existence, he experienced our worries, fears, disappointments, and stresses. Jesus knew he would be ill-equipped to handle it all without God's gifts of calm and peace. His method was to step away—to the desert, to the garden, underneath a fig tree, or walking the seashore. In quietness and stillness, like Jesus, we can replenish ourselves and rebuild our reserves of hope.

A peaceful existence requires incredible intentionality. Commit to a personal "monastery" experience once each day. Watch what a difference it makes.

Prince of Peace,

I long for our conversations in the quiet.
You settle me.
It's comforting to know You experienced all that I face on
Earth.
The angst, the worry, the doubt,
the unpredictable, the unmerciful, the broken.
See how I fight for control over my today and tomorrow.
Bless me with a dose of Your mysterious peace,
the peace I will never find in the world
or manifest for myself.
How it soothes every wrinkle in the fabric of me.
I am transformed.
I can do things I thought impossible,
I find courage to meet the hard days,
the world receives a gentler me,
I find again my hope.
I need to trust You—with everything—once and for all.
Eternity is already stamped on my passport,
and for those I love.
Let this ultimate truth give me the sweet peace I long for.
Nothing compares to resting under Your wing.

Amen.

Create a Monastery Moment in Grand Central Station

HOW DIFFICULT IT is to get a moment of silence as the conductor of six kids, four dogs, one husband, and two jobs! My life is 24/7 Grand Central Station. If I am not careful, I become a spinning top. Monks take periodic vows of silence and solitude. No talking, reading, or writing, and certainly no social media. They refer to the time as noble silence. It is a time-out so the mind, body, and spirit can rest, replenish, and realign. Silence helps to clear the noise in the mind and release the tension in the body. An extra bonus is breakthrough creativity and much better problem-solving.

A monastic experience can happen in your car, sitting on your porch, lying in your bed, or walking alone in nature. Leave your phone, children, TV, dogs, and to-do lists behind and escape through the metaphorical monastery doors. Give yourself fifteen minutes of unscheduled quiet once a day. I like the resting savasana yoga pose that typically closes a yoga class:

Take a comfortable position lying flat on your back, either on a mat or bed, your arms and palms spread wide and open, with a pillow under your knees for support. Take a couple of deep breaths through the nose and out the mouth, and then lie there, perfectly still and quiet. Relish the peace.

14
Waiting

We could never learn to be brave and patient,
if there were only joy in the world.
—HELEN KELLER

I wait for the Lord, my whole being waits,
and in his word, I put my hope.
—PSALM 130:5 (NIV)

It was Sunday morning. I arose as usual to read the lectionary at church and somehow knocked the Bible clear off the pulpit. It hit the hardwood floor with an unholy thud. Gasps and giggles could be heard from the front two rows. Next, I forgot which scripture I was reading. All of this transpired in front of over four hundred congregants. It was not my best day. The truth—I was suffering silently from the universal human condition of waiting for something that would either make or break my heart.

Have you been there—that unnerving purgatory of waiting, where you are desperate to stop or fast-forward time to receive a desired outcome for yourself or someone you love? At any given moment, we are all waiting for the beginning or the ending of something. We wait for dreams to come true. We wait for answers to prayers. We wait to hear "I love you" or "I'm sorry." We wait for medical tests and their results. We wait for relief from betrayal, heartbreak, pain, and grief. We wait for new life, new possibilities, new adventures. We wait for death. We wait for heaven.

Waiting, in my experience, can feel like you are crossing a black hole on a tightrope or like you are about to crest a new and exciting vista.

In that embarrassing Bible-dropping moment, I was waiting for a significant medical scan for my daughter. I was on day two of a five-day waiting bender. To say the least, the waiting had turned me upside down and sideways. I was in the grind of worry and doing my best to muscle through.

The tension in waiting is unavoidable and will leave us, at different times in our lives, uncomfortably vulnerable, tender, even desperate. But impatience does not change outcomes. It is humbling when we realize we cannot strong-arm our destinies.

Anger and disappointment with God are to be expected. But much scarier is the thought of blazing the uncertain, unpredictable trail apart from God. Still, there will be questions and scenarios that we will wait for with patience and faith but not receive answers on this side of heaven. Cosmic timing often does not match our own. Sometimes we have to bravely let go of the life we planned in order to step into the destiny God imagined for us. In the mucky trenches of waiting and sweating it out, faith is revealed. Our capacity to hope without certainty expands. Remember, God is focused on the long view, where love becomes the final punctuation on our stories. Our work is to trust and surrender and then do it again and again.

I am beginning to understand that waiting is a spiritual discipline— one that requires determination and perseverance, and cannot be done alone. We wait on God together.

Holy and Loving God,

More than ever, I feel the poignancy of being human
and—my need of Your saving grace.
Please help me make my way.

You call me to look for glimmers of hope
no matter how dark and uncertain my present reality.

Teach me how to hold the sorrow
and the joy in me at once.
And release the fear, so hope can flood the tender in me.
You promise that even if I cannot see it,
Your mysterious Love
is holding me together.
All will come together for good.

Reveal Your calming presence to me
in nature, in chapel candlelight,
in the faces of loved ones and even strangers.
Keep whispering this Truth to me—
I have you.
Love will prevail.

A most grateful Amen.

Help for Waiting

(These Are Also Helpful in the Province of Grief)

INSTEAD OF UNRAVELING during periods of waiting, take action. Focus on taming the fight-or-flight instinct that is so unhealthy for mind, body, and spirit. Avoid the black hole of what-if scenarios that often lead us to the worst common denominator. Meet fear and uncertainty with faith and hope. Following are ways to have compassion for yourself in the hard waiting. Try one each day of the week, or maybe, like me, sometimes your salvation is doing all of them in a single day.

1. Reach out to a select group of people whom you trust and share your burden. There is relief in knowing you are not alone and someone else is lifting you in prayer.

2. Exercise with a good sweat to release anxiety and help regain calmness and control in the face of the unknown. So many hormones and emotions, many of which are anxiety-charged, flow through us as we wait.

3. Find ways to love yourself well. Listen to music, take a lavender Epsom salt soak, savor a cup of herbal tea, light candles, apply scented calming oils, wrap yourself in a weighted blanket, or cook a comforting meal.

4. Journal your thoughts. Once they are on paper, the fear loses some of its power. We then can formulate healthier responses, a "hope in action" stratagem.

5. Get outside into nature! I have made some serious ruts walking the paths at Radnor Lake here in Nashville. I always return to my life and the waiting with more balance and increased hope.

6. Read the Psalms, especially Psalm 23. They provide a model for "waiting on God." They encourage me to hang on and trust that God will come through.

7. Pray without ceasing. Be bold and ask God for what you need. It is comforting to know that I am not alone and without resources. There is a spiritual reality larger than myself and my circumstances working for good on my behalf that I can connect to.

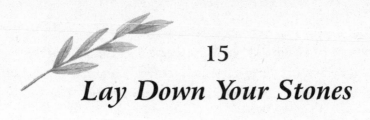

15

Lay Down Your Stones

To love is to be in communion with the other
and to discover in that other the spark of God.
—PAULO COELHO

Above all, love each other deeply,
because love covers over a multitude of sins.
—1 PETER 4:8 (NIV)

On a trip to France, my family and I happened upon a beautiful hiking trail through olive groves and fields of poppies called *La Mur de la Peste*. This trail is a twenty-seven-kilometers-long meander along an ancient crumbling stone wall. A plaque from 1720 lies near the trailhead, which explains that this stout wall had been a barrier dividing the south and north of France. Over three centuries ago, a doomed ship had sailed into the southern port of Marseille carrying fine silks, but also bubonic plague. In a few months over fifty thousand French men, women, and children died from this disease. Panicking, King Louis ordered the wall to be built to keep *la peste* from reaching the heart of France.

They somehow believed this wall, one that could be easily hopped over, could actually stop the spread of the bubonic plague.

Today we build walls too—physical ones but also metaphorical ones. Neither solve any problems. At the first sign of possible danger or heartbreak, we start assembling the barricades. Unkind words, turned shoulders, cold silence, avoidance, and downright meanness all become our stones for a wall to separate us. Righteously, we claim it is in the name of self-preservation. But the truth is we are pridefully denying a chance for reconciliation and understanding. This resentment and selfishness are the worst kind of plague because they take us down silently from the inside.

All of us have been misunderstood, unjustly hurt, and sorely disappointed by those in our inner circle. Where else but in our relationships do we reveal the best and worst of ourselves? It's in these day-to-day exchanges that we expose how petty, shortsighted, or selfish we can be—but also how merciful, empathetic, and loving we have the capacity to be as well. Not one of us is beyond judgment . . . or mercy!

We could all use a refresher on how to see the world through another's eyes, reading another's heart. It sounds simple, but when we suspend our reality for just a moment to slip into that of another, we likely might be stupefied: "That's how they were feeling? No wonder they acted that way."

Every day we have the choice to meet the world from our flaws or from our glory.

I am beginning to understand Jesus' wisdom when, after Peter asks him how many times must he forgive his brother, Jesus responds, "[Forgive] not seven times, but, I tell you, seventy-seven times."* Forgiveness requires serious spiritual muscle, and we have to keep exercising it for it to grow strong. We can say to the one who hurt us, "I forgive you," but real and lasting forgiveness, the kind that sets us free, must manifest from within us. Let's not wait until the hourglass is empty to choose mercy for ourselves and for those we love right now. Tear down your internal walls of self-protection and open your heart. If you do this, others will follow your direction.

---

* Matthew 18:22, NRSV

Beloved,

I humbly approach your altar today,
to confess the truths of my heart.
You see in secret my imperfections and fragile faith.
All that I have done and left undone.
Quick to judge, stingy with forgiveness—
a stonewall of hubris.
I bear no angel's wings.
Untangle me from my ego.
Teach me how to forgive myself and then others,
to choose love,
even, and especially,
when my pride is against it.
Today is a new day in my mission of Love.
I will gather my courage to give my heart away.
Every time I do this,
a little piece of me is redeemed,
and I move one step closer to
Your kingdom.

Amen.

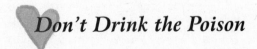

Don't Drink the Poison

WHAT IF OUR relationships are our spiritual legacy? What if the cosmos is tallying how well we forgive and how respectfully we treat those we claim to love? Life's value ultimately depends on the quality of love given and received over a lifetime. Let's ask ourselves, "What kind of fingerprints are we leaving on others' hearts?" Have we built unseen walls of pride, resentment, and hurt? Remove them so love, peace, and freedom can take their place.

There is a difficult someone in your life right now who is occupying some of your soul space that could be filled with joy. You need to release them. Take a peace rose to them, or just call them on the phone. Harboring resentment is a joy-killer. There's an adage often attributed to Nelson Mandela that says it so well: "Resentment is like drinking poison and then hoping it will kill your enemies." I challenge you to forgive that difficult person in your life. Sometimes it takes many times to finally let it go. Whenever you think of the person or replay what they did to you, pray for them by name. Keep doing this until joy fills again your heart space.

16

Tree Hugger

He who loves is a participant in the being of God.
—MARTIN LUTHER KING, JR.

Live a life of love.
—EPHESIANS 5:2 (ERV)

I have always admired trees: the prehistoric ginkgo, the gigantic angel oak, the sweet Southern magnolia, the fragrant olive tree, the elegant weeping willow. I often speak to God beneath their leafy branches because I sense God's gentle attention there. I fell in love with my husband while hiking Sewanee's famous Perimeter Trail beneath a towering fortress of pine trees. For my fortieth birthday, David gifted me with pairs of apple, pear, plum, and cherry trees. The cover illustration for my first book, *Alma Gloria and the Olive Tree,* sums up my evergreen devotion perfectly with a tree carved with a heart.

You could say I am a true tree hugger.

Trees symbolize hope for me, as they seem to take the long view of life. Serene instead of reactive, trees focus on the things that matter. They ground themselves deeply in an intricate root system, arrow-point themselves to the sun, practice patience in the face of changing seasons, and keep a stoic eye on their legacies. In the stillness of the forest, I have become convinced that trees have figured out the secret: It takes every kind of love to make this planet turn.

Now, you might ask yourself, "Has Farrell gone off the deep end, anthropomorphizing trees?" But what if I told you that trees have feelings and a capacity to show love? In Peter Wohlleben's *The Hidden Life of Trees*, we discover that not only do trees smell and taste, but they "talk" to each other! Trees have families and a circle of friends. They store memories and make their own green plans for the future. But more importantly, trees take care of one another.

If one tree is ill, all the surrounding trees will send sugar and nourishment through their connected roots to revive that tree. All are accounted for—the orphans, widows, elderly. Did you know trees register pain? If an invader such as an insect, bird, or human comes into the area, the trees immediately send out root alerts to warn the other trees to take precautions. Trees intuit that they cannot survive alone and hence take part in the symbiotic community of the forest.

The fact is, tree and human alike, we need each other. Statistics show that isolation and its ensuing loneliness is a secret killer. Meaningful living happens in community. I wish to start a Love Your Neighborhood campaign. There have been significant examples in my own life where neighbors, either geographical or connected by work or faith, have shown me love, even "saved the day" for me.

During my son's cancer, we were living in an apartment building in New York City. We didn't know our neighbors except for a passing hello in the elevator. Eventually, word spread, and people became aware of our son's health. One day, I received a knock on my apartment door. It was Mary, empty laundry basket in hand, from down the hall. For the next eight months, she did my laundry every week. The baby clothes, my sheets and towels, all arrived cleaned, pressed, and smelling of lavender. I will never forget her kindness.

I see a blueprint of love in nature, a radical and divine system that extends across all of creation. It operates on love, given and received. We are designed to shepherd one another. It's genius, really, that human beings and saplings alike are wired for compassionate sacrifice. The archetype metaphor of "forest" (marriage, family, neighborhood, community, church, world) is only as strong as the selfless heart of every tree and creature living within it.

If you are struggling to answer these questions: Why am I here? What is my purpose? How do I live more soulfully? Take direction from the trees. They are sage teachers. Our arboreal role models are fulfilling their destinies in the forest by listening, protecting, showing kindness, and loving every tree with whom they share a segment of life. This is our spiritual work too. If we do nothing else in our short time span, let it be said that we overcommunicated love with those who crossed "roots" with us.

Life Giver,

Sometimes I wish I could live in the trees,
where it's quiet,
and I feel Your embrace.
I can think, or not,
and just be.
My secrets slip out and lose their power over me
in Your evergreen cathedral.
I carve this prayer into the massive oak:
"Be with me whenever, however, forever."
The tears come; smiles too.

A rosary of names is quietly entrusted to You.
Take care of those I love.
Hope comes in tiny
glimmers breaking through
Your eternal canopy.

A grateful Amen.

The Perfect Roasted Chicken

This week, discover your own evergreen altar in nature, a safe place to go and be heard. Return to the world, taking wisdom from the trees, and consider how you might nourish your own community this week. Loving your neighbor is actually quite simple: Make another feel seen and loved. We are here because someone needs our love! As Jesus says, we only gain our lives when we are willing to give them away for others. In the spirit of my Love Your Neighborhood campaign, pick a desk mate at work, your ninety-seven-year-old homebound neighbor down the street, the person you share the pew with at church every Sunday, your partner, a child, mother-in-law, pet. Surprise them with coffee, homemade bread, dog treats, a mason jar of flowers, even take their trash cans up the driveway for them. Or how about you deliver my famous Perfect Roasted Chicken?

This is one of those recipes that every home chef should commit to memory. Although simple to prepare, it is full of flavor. Serve with a big green salad, mashed potatoes, rice or couscous, and a baguette, and you can collect your three Michelin stars!

Ingredients

1 whole organic chicken, 4–5 lbs
olive oil
kosher salt and ground pepper
herbes de Provence
2 lemons, washed, split in quarters

1 onion, split in quarters
1 cup Mediterranean olives
　　(a mélange of olives with pits)
4–6 fresh thyme sprigs

Directions

Preheat oven to 425°F. Start with an organic 4- to 5-pound chicken. Wash thoroughly, inside and out. Pat dry. You need to cook the chicken in a pot that has a lid to encourage the best flavors. Give a light covering of olive oil to the bottom of your pot. Generously cover the chicken inside and out with olive oil, kosher salt, ground pepper, and herbes de Provence. Cut 1 lemon into quarters; 2 quarters go inside the cavity of the bird, 2 go in the pot. Cut an onion into quarters; again, 2 go inside the chicken, 2 in the pot. Pour your olives into the pot. Flip bird breast-down to cook. Decorate the top of the chicken with fresh thyme sprigs. (You have no idea how yummy the gravy is with the lemon, thyme, and olives—it's a work of art in itself!)

Cover the pot and put in the preheated oven. Leave covered to cook for an hour and a half. My butcher recommends a chicken cook 20 minutes for each pound it weighs. The secret is in basting the chicken in its own gravy halfway through cooking, and again at the end. I usually turn off the oven and baste it a couple of times while I am making my mashed potatoes. Voilà! You'll have a roasted chicken to rival any Michelin-starred French chef and a very happy neighbor!

17

Cut a New Destiny

Still, a great deal of light falls on everything.
—VINCENT VAN GOGH

Behold I am making all things new . . . Write this down,
for these words are trustworthy and true.
—REVELATION 21:5 (ESV)

Most would agree that Henri Matisse was an extraordinary painter. For over half a century, this French artist created a canon of inspired art. What many don't know is that he spent the last ten years of his life an invalid, confined to a wheelchair, and housebound. Due to several near-fatal illnesses, Matisse could never paint again. He certainly could have quietly given in to his fate. But that just wasn't his way.

Matisse believed that to live and to create was a human being's greatest honor. His body might have given out, but not his spirit.

He traded his paintbrush and easel for a pair of scissors and brightly colored papers. Matisse literally "cut" a new destiny for himself. The artist spent his last days cutting colorful shapes and images from paper. By creatively pinning the cutouts together, suddenly he had stars glowing, figures dancing, and flowers blooming.

Critics championed his new art form. It became clear that the aging Matisse was living the ancient wisdom: "Become like a child again to enter the kingdom of heaven."* The art of his later life radiates a childlike wonder that is contagious. Matisse compared cutting shapes from paper to flying. He said, "An artist must never be a prisoner of himself."

One of Matisse's final commissions was for a chapel in the south of France. He considered it his finest masterpiece. Hundreds of cut-out shapes and dramatic colors converged in the stained glass windows and upon the altar. His work was glory incarnate. It was his tribute to the One who gave him life, love, and creativity in the first place!

Too easily we allow circumstances in life to shut us down. There are plenty of reasons to throw in the towel, raise the white flag of surrender, harden our hearts, and bench our souls. But as Matisse found, we are much more than our fragile bodies or our circumstances. Is there something in your life that needs to be reconsidered? Maybe like Matisse you need to get creative and try a new approach. There is no time like the present to cut a new destiny.

Beloved,

No one knows me like You do; beast and beauty.
Luminous but many chinks in my armor.
Inside this gargoyle lives an angel, right?
In the deep of my deep,
I long to be Your noble servant,
but the coil of life trips me up all the time.
First, it's the busyness;
I skim only the top off of life in my rush
to be here, there, and everywhere.

* Matthew 18:3

Slow me down,
steep my soul with grace.
Second, it's the worry;
I give it power, and it tightens like
an unwanted corset around my soul.
You know I am tender.
Make me resilient when the arrows come.
Remind me the right way is always love's way.
Cut a pattern of redemption in my story, please.
Mercy given, mercy received—set me free.
Point me in the direction of the kingdom of heaven.

Amen.

Chicky Parmesan

During the unprecedented COVID-19 pandemic, when life as we knew it and enjoyed it shut down, creativity became our salvation. My seven-year-old son, Percy, and I decided to turn lemons into lemonade. We filmed a plucky, homespun cooking show each night entitled *Mama! Let's Cook!* Two years later, in matching aprons, with Percy telling jokes while whipping fresh cream for a strawberry dessert and my daughter Elise giggling behind the camera, I am reminded all is never completely lost. Sometimes we just have to get creative to find our joy again. A favorite episode was our Italian Friday night dinner of chicken parmesan with a quick and simple arugula salad and Percy's take on *cacio e pepe* (a.k.a. buttered noodles).

Ingredients

4 chicken breasts, cut in half
   crosswise
3 tbsp olive oil, plus more
   for drizzling
sea salt
freshly ground pepper
2 tsp fresh rosemary leaves,
   chopped
2 tsp fresh thyme leaves, chopped

1 jar of marinara sauce
8 oz buttercup or mozzarella
   cheese, shredded
1 cup Parmesan (½ for chicken,
   ½ for the pasta)
1 box pasta of your choice
2 tbsp grass-fed butter
1 cup fresh spinach, roughly
   chopped

Directions

Preheat oven to 400°F. Put the chicken breasts between two pieces of parchment or wax paper and flatten with a rolling pin to uniform thickness of ⅓ to ¾ inches (optional but recommended). Drizzle chicken breasts with olive oil and sprinkle with salt, pepper, rosemary, and thyme. In a large cast-iron skillet of your choosing (I use my Le Creuset large, deep frying pan), heat 2–3 tablespoons of olive oil over medium heat. Add the chicken and cook until slightly golden, about 5 minutes on each side. Remove from heat, drain excess liquid, and pour marinara sauce over chicken. Scatter your 2 cheeses on top and cook until bubbling, either on the stovetop or in the oven, around 15 minutes. Cook a pasta of your choice, in salted water, to al dente. Stir in 2 tbsp butter, ½ cup Parmesan, fresh spinach, kosher salt, and fresh-ground pepper. Serve chicken with pasta and a side of broccoli.

18

Eyes Peeled

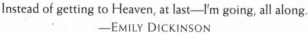

Instead of getting to Heaven, at last—I'm going, all along.
—EMILY DICKINSON

Truly, the Lord is in this place and I did not know it!
—GENESIS 28:16 (NABRE)

Whenever I jog around Radnor Lake, I know I'll be greeted by amazing flora and fauna. One particular morning, however, I was greeted instead by a row of cameras with super-large lenses lined up along the edge of the lake. They belonged to photographers who call themselves the "Radnor Paparazzi." With their heads tilted to the sky, they clearly had something extraordinary in their sights. Curious, I stopped running to see what all the excitement was about, but for the life of me, I could not spy what had captured their attention.

"Is it a sage owl, a bald eagle, a blue heron, an ancient snapping turtle, the elusive otter?" I asked.

One of the older gentlemen chuckled and then pointed up into the branches of a tall, majestic maple tree.

"I don't see anything," I said.

"It's dark gray and the size of a golf ball!" he said.

"The size of a golf ball?" I exclaimed.

There was utter silence, his eyes focused in rapt anticipation.

"It's a hummingbird's nest! You're lucky if you see one in your whole lifetime. A needle in a haystack, you might say."

"Or a miracle," whisperéd the gentleman with the largest lens.

A hummingbird's nest is considered a true wonder of the world. Minute in size and incredibly well concealed, it's very rarely seen by the human eye.

Dave, leader of the Radnor Paps, invited me to view this phenomenon through his lens. There, in all her glory, was a mother hummingbird. The size of my pointer finger, weighing less than a nickel, and with wings flapping over two hundred times per second, she was hovering over her exquisite nest. Mr. Dave showed me pictures captured over the previous week with his ultra-high-powered lens. One of the mother feeding nectar, beak to beak, to her two-week-old babies. Another of the mother hovering, her wings moving so fast they were only captured as a blur on the film. My favorite was the one of the babes trying out their wings for the first time.

I turned to the rest of the group and asked, "How in the world did you see something this tiny and so magnificent?"

The only lady in the bunch piped up: "It's amazing what God will show you if you just keep your eyes peeled."

Sometimes the tiniest glimpses of God can literally save us. Thankfully, as the poet Gerard Manley Hopkins wrote, "The world is charged with the grandeur of God." A feasible spiritual quest is to search for and find a glimmer of divinity in every given day. I believe it's the secret to increasing our inner reserves of hope.

The Radnor Paparazzi came every day until the birds fledged. I asked what happens next.

"Then we will look for our next wonder," a twinkling-eyed elder gentleman in a baseball cap offered with a child's enthusiasm.

I wanted to join the group!

Imagine—in the midst of hurricanes, addiction, infertility, broken relationships, and loss, we could become members of the Divine Paparazzi. We could set out every day, with eyes peeled, to discover one inch of beauty, one tiny revelation of our Creator with the power to save us!

Dear God,

This morning began quite ordinary,
as miracles do.
A walk in the emerald wood.
Until the skies opened
and the Spirit revealed Herself
twirling in the wind.
A squirrel, a pair of chipmunks,
and a blue jay stopped
what they were doing
waiting in rapt attention
as I received a raindrop baptism.
How quickly the ordinary can become sacramental.
Today I received a raindrop blessing,
Your mighty trees as my holy witnesses.
You must have known
I was due a transformation.
I shall not be returning home the same.

Amen.

#InchofBeauty

IT IS EASY to slip into believing the world is all doom and gloom. We must actively search for proof that life is more than good and remarkably hopeful. Take a photo of your daily inch of beauty. Text the photo to a friend with the hashtags #inchofbeauty, #Godishere, #liveinhope. Make it a daily discipline to document God's presence in the world. I guarantee it will inch you and those you love closer to the soulfull life.

19

Ready to Fly

Faith is stepping out into the unknown with nothing to guide us
but a hand just beyond our grasp.
—FREDERICK BUECHNER

Trust steadily in God, hope unswervingly, love extravagantly.
—1 CORINTHIANS 13:13 (MSG)

Several years ago, after a picnic lunch, my four older children were set free to ride their bikes around the circumference of Radnor Lake. Pedaling fiercely in their dust was my younger son, Percy, trying his best to keep up on his little blue bike with training wheels. He announced, "I'm ready to ride with them, Mom!"

I knew this rite of passage would come with some crocodile tears, scraped knees, stormy frustration, and moments of real fear. But there was an unmistakable look of determination in my son's eyes. Percy was indeed ready to fly! My sister, Belle, suggested we start the project on the Radio Flyer Glider, a mini bike with no pedals. Percy could push fast with his feet on the ground until he gained enough momentum to lift them and let the bike fly. That little Glider was the trick! Percy found his balance and a happy glimpse of soaring. The next stage was a real bike. Before long, he was ready for the trails on his big brother's mountain bike.

Learning to ride a bike is a beautiful metaphor for the progression of faith. Scientists have discovered that there is a special area in the brain's cerebellum that permanently imprints learned experiences such as riding a bike. I believe the same process happens for one's soul when it experiences the divine reality within and all around. With every experience of God in earthly time and space, we create soul muscle memories. And our faith grows.

Faith begins with a twinkling suspicion deep within us that there is more here than meets the eye. Our material existence isn't all there is. We are inherently connected to God, a sacred reality. Curiosity and necessity inspire the pursuit of a spiritual life that supports our mortal existence and ensures our lives have eternal consequence.

I imagine my faith as a marvelous but invisible umbilical cord that connects my soul to God. Regardless of my earthly circumstances, my fears, even my mortality, it sustains my being. Earth becomes the training ground to test its strength and elasticity. Every time I love, forgive, create beauty, practice trust in God, and hope in the face of despair, I transcend our broken world and my faith miraculously expands.

Paul's definition of Christian faith is simple: "Faith is the assurance of things hoped for, the conviction of things not seen."* Look inward. There is a mysterious, mystical "love pact" between one's soul and God. God connects us to the essentials that our souls long for and the world has no power to give.

We need faith like we need oxygen. Life is hopeless without it. We will fail in this challenging world if we rely just on ourselves. But let's be honest, learning to ride a bike and keeping the faith are not an easy Sunday afternoon ride in the park. My own connection with God waxes and wanes. In our secular, self-reliant culture, faithfulness is a challenge. The capacity of my faith completely depends on the degree to which I trust

---

*   Hebrews 11:1, NRSV

God and operate in the world from my soul. At its best, my faith gives me the peace and courage I need to handle life's fragility and daily defeats.

I was relieved when I read the surprising confession from Mother Teresa in her book *Come Be My Light*, that for years she prayed to what she described as a black void, receiving no assurance or comfort. Nevertheless, she kept the faith. This gives me hope. I appreciate her truthfulness. Faith is a daily practice of trust. The most authentic prayer I know is "Dear God, I believe. Help my unbelief."* No matter the path's twists and turns or the seasons of light and darkness, we must keep pedaling. Our ultimate destination is secure.

Faith is more than just a life preserver on Earth, it's also our opportunity to experience what the German theologian Rudolf Otto called the "mysterium tremendum," where Heaven breaks through, and life is experienced as marvelously sacred. I don't know where you are on your journey; maybe doubt is having its way with you, or you are just hanging on, or maybe you feel God as close as your heartbeat and as near as your breath. Regardless, make this the year your faith expands. Frederick Buechner wrote, "When faith stops changing and growing, it dies on its feet." Commit to discovering new ways to pull on the sacred tether and experience more of God. For me, I have experienced a new energy in my own spiritual life in reading Eugene Peterson's *The Message*, a beautiful and approachable translation of the Bible.

I have yet to master completely trusting God's providence in my life. But the glimpses of God, those "soaring" moments when the divine reality becomes my present reality, keep me pedaling toward a promised horizon.

---

* See Mark 9:24.

Beloved,

Like a wily horse in the ring of life:
I am green, unpredictable.
Although tethered to heaven by a luminous rein,
You would never know it by the way I canter life's course.
Bucking Your love right out of the saddle,
so foolish and sure that I know the right way.

Can You put me back on the correct lead?
Train me in Your love gospel.
Teach me grace.
To be noble, pure of heart, merciful.

I long to
live by faith,
reflecting Your love in the world,
salvation, my epilogue.

A grateful Amen.

Praying the Examen

IN THE SPIRIT of expanding our faith, I recommend trying St. Ignatius's Examen. In the fifteenth century, St. Ignatius of Loyola, the founder of the order of the Jesuits, created a daily spiritual exercise to take a meaningful accounting of our lives. The Examen is a five-step process that begins with spying instances in our day when we have been aware of divinity in our midst and ends with asking the Divine Presence to be with us tomorrow as we rise to meet another day. Practicing the Examen keeps us in the habit of noticing the unmistakable presence of God in our daily, ordinary lives.

The Examen

Step One: Ask God to be with you. I believe we are always in the presence of God, but when we ask God to draw close to us, our present reality is freshly experienced as sacred.

Step Two: Review the events of your day for when you were certain of God's presence. Maybe it was an experience of beauty in nature, in created art, or in relationship with another. Where did you feel hopeful or inspired? I confess, during the challenging seasons, especially ones weighted with grief or when the path forward feels scary and uncertain, I spend more time here in Step Two, looking for any light in the darkness, any signs of hope to keep stepping forward.

Step Three: Next, do an accounting of the people, places, and exchanges where you were too busy, too self-consumed, too fearful to see God at work or allow yourself to be a conduit of God's presence. Where did I not show up with my best self? Where did I miss an opportunity to increase goodness on my watch? Where did I cast a shadow when I could have radiated light?

Step Four: Ask for forgiveness from God, your family, friends, others, even yourself. Trespasses confessed are forgiven. We are set free to try again. And again.

Step Five: Invite God to show up again tomorrow. Have your eyes and heart open. Commit to looking for signs of divinity in your daily life. Carry love forward on your watch. Close with a prayer of thanks for where you are now and where you hope to be going.

20

Press On

Christ with me,
Christ before me,
Christ behind me,
Christ in me,
Christ beneath me,
Christ above me.
—St. Patrick's Breastplate Prayer

Now faith is the substance of things hoped for,
the evidence of things not seen.
—Hebrews 11:1 (KJV)

The mysterious disappearance of the Teton mountains was all the talk in Jackson Hole in the summer of 2021. My family and I took a trip there, and right off the plane, we looked for the Grand, the tallest of the Teton peaks, soaring to an impressive 13,775 feet. Strangely, though, it was missing for most of our ten-day visit. A tourist in town bemoaned that he had traveled across the country in his RV to see the biggest Teton, a natural wonder in North America, only to leave with just a postcard. The Tetons were there, of course. They were just temporarily hidden behind a cloud veil, a result of the unprecedented western forest fires that summer. Sometimes it feels like God has disappeared behind a cloud veil too, and our faith is tested.

The experience of faith can be described in three words: wonder, patience, expectation. **Wonder** is the awe of knowing in your "soul bones" that God is in us and always surrounding us. **Patience** is the spiritual discipline to accept seasons of divine silence and human doubt. **Expectation** is anticipating—trusting—in the next moment God will show up for us.

Every human being will spend time, maybe even desperate seasons, in darkness and uncertainty. God seems absent, and life is experienced as brutish, unrelenting. Few alleluias and amens are spoken. The real work of faith begins in this wilderness. Bravely, relentlessly, practice hope until the clouds pass. God won't pull an "Elvis" and leave the stage of our lives, just as the Tetons have not disappeared in their over nine million years!

How do we pick up the bread-crumb trail of hope when the Teton Mountains and God seem missing?

We must do a better job *looking* for God and the good in our midst. When life is not experienced as sun-glistened mountaintops, we must commit to spiritual disciplines that will sustain us until the clouds part. Sometimes this calls for a return to traditions and rituals. I lean into my faith community, music, Bible study, the sacraments, and fellowship. Nature is also my chapel, a place where I feel God's presence and utter goodness. Remember and reflect on past chapters of your life when God showed up for you. Tuck into scriptures such as Psalm 139 and Jeremiah 29:11 for encouragement and call on friends and family for support.

Daily as we plot our way out of the wilderness, our cloud veil lifts. God proves that love can be trusted over and over again.

Wherever you are right now—a place of wonder, practicing patience, or on the edge of your seat—press on.

Guardian of my heart,

Did you clock out?
Are you napping?
Have you finally thrown Your hands up,
the world too lost, too broken?
I'm still here, in the wilderness
waiting for You.
Doubt visits,
makes me squirm.
If there were ever a time
for Your angels to rush in,
it is now.
Send a mistral into these dry bones.
I will open my front door,
lay out the welcome mat,
pull the screens off every window,
and chimney-sweep the hearth
for Your Spirit to find a way in—
Won't You stay a while?
Sometimes I catch a shimmer of You
from the corner of my eye.
Why can it not be all Light, all the time?
Why must we hurt beneath Heaven's rim?
I am determined to connect the sacred dots,
before my Hourglass is empty.
I am going to love who and what is right in front of me.

That is when You show up.
And God, I don't say it enough—I love you.

A grateful Amen.

Mediterranean Chicken

Gathering around the table with the people you love for a good meal helps the clouds lift. And often physical nourishment is exactly what we need to press on. The inspiration for this recipe came after a day of hiking in the Tetons. Could there be any better combination than olives, tomatoes, cucumbers, feta cheese, fresh oregano, fresh mint, basil, lemon, and olive oil? It is one of the top requests for dinner at our house. It serves my family of eight.

Ingredients

8 skinless, boneless chicken breasts
1 cup high-quality olive oil, divided
juice from 2 lemons, divided
6 tsp fresh oregano, chopped
6 tsp fresh sage, chopped
2 garlic cloves, pressed
½ cup fresh basil, chopped
2 tbsp fresh mint, chopped
salt and pepper

1 large seedless cucumber,
    peeled and diced
1 cup pitted green and Kalamata
    olives, chopped
1 bushel grape tomatoes, chopped
    (I use heirloom when I can get
    them, for mix of colors)
1 cup feta cheese, crumbled

Directions

Score the top of your chicken breasts and pound to ⅓-inch thickness. Divide chicken breasts into two Ziploc bags. In a separate bowl, whisk together the marinade of ½ cup olive oil, juice from 1 lemon, 6 teaspoons oregano, 6 teaspoons sage, and pressed garlic in a small bowl. Season the dressing with salt and pepper to taste. Split marinade into the two bags. Coat chicken breasts in marinade and chill in refrigerator for 1–3 hours.

In a separate bowl, create your "knock your socks off" tapenade for the chicken. Combine tomatoes, olives, cucumbers, basil, mint, remaining lemon juice, ½ cup olive oil, and feta cheese. Season with salt and pepper.

Sauté chicken breasts with marinade until cooked through, about 3 minutes per side. Transfer to cutting board and slice at an angle. Spoon tapenade onto chicken. Serve with a simple green salad and crunchy olive bread!

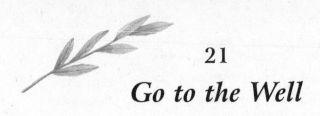

21

Go to the Well

Once the soul awakens, the search begins and you can never go
back. From then on, you are inflamed with a special longing that
will never again let you linger in the lowlands of complacency
and partial fulfillment. The eternal makes you urgent.
—JOHN O'DONOHUE

For he will command his angels concerning you
to guard you in all your ways.
—PSALM 91:11 (NRSV)

In 1858, in Lourdes, France, it was reported that the Virgin Mary miraculously appeared eighteen times to a poor shepherd girl named
Bernadette. In one of the visions, the Virgin Mary caused a spring to burst
forth inside the grotto, once a lowly shelter for pigs. Mary directed Bernadette to drink from and bathe in these special waters. Since that day, an
astonishing number of people have reported healings after visiting the
spring. There have been so many claims that the Catholic Church estab-
lished an international medical committee in 1905—composed of the
leading scientists, doctors, and theologians of the world—to study and
document the claims of healing. Many have been validated.

Every year millions of people make a pilgrimage to this sacred water-
ing hole nestled at the base of the Pyrenees. They come for the water. And
hopefully they leave with so much more.

My first pilgrimage to Lourdes was nineteen years ago. I had received
in the mail a bottle of Lourdes holy water for my son Charlie, then under-

going treatment for cancer. My husband, mom, and I made a pact that one day we would go ourselves. We did go, and since then, Lourdes has become a spiritual touchstone for me, a place where I feel the presence of God. I leave with a renewed faith and soul-deep peace. I don't think I am alone in my curiosity and longing to experience something deeper here on Earth. Every single soul craves experiences of the eternal.

In the summer of 2019, I made my third pilgrimage to Lourdes. In the biggest heat wave to hit France in a hundred years, I carried my empty plastic gallon jug, emblazoned with a stamp of the Virgin Mary, to the grotto. On this particular day, I was one in a multitude of seekers. I joined the morning procession through the gates alongside an elderly couple holding hands, in matching wheelchairs; a pair of Chinese priests; a foursome of Italian nuns, all smiles and rosaries twirling; a band of villagers from Chile in matching T-shirts; and finally a woman from Africa, regal in a colorful tapestry headdress. All of us were making our faithful way to the well for the holy water, empty bottles in hand.

My first stop was at the baths, where you immerse in the water. The wait to go in took over three hours, because the sick, the disabled, and children have priority. Here I met Irish Mary. We sat on the wooden benches outside the baths, waiting our turn together. She gave me a hug as if we had known each other all our lives. Mary is a seventy-eight-year-old nurse from County Cork, Ireland. This was her thirty-third pilgrimage to Lourdes. This time I believe she came for me. Our conversation took a theological turn toward the end of the day. "O Farrell, love," she said in that musical accent of hers, "why have you come to Lourdes, with that gallon jug of yours? What do you need?" It took me a moment to answer the question. "I guess, Mary, I have come for what the world can't give me. I have come for peace. I have come to refill on hope. I have come to feel God's presence."

Mary's response: "Knock, and the door will be opened to you."

Mary and I parted ways at the entry to the baths. I went one way and she went the other, but not before she flashed me a knowing smile and said, "O Farrell, wouldn't it be grand if every day was like today? Showing up with our souls, not our egos. We'd be kind, kind, kind [she said it three times] to one another. It would be mercy given instead of so much judgment. There would be peace knowing everything will be okay, for all of us." And then she disappeared behind the blue curtain separating the bathing chambers. What creative ways God has of communicating to us; that day it was with an Irish lilt and twinkling green eyes.

For over two thousand years, Christians have embarked on pilgrimages to make a change, for inner peace, to find healing, or to achieve a new intimacy with God. Always, it is less about the destination and so much more about the journey and transformation of the seeking heart. Sometimes we have to step away from our routines to feel something holy. In the Gospel of Matthew, Jesus says, "Go to your room, shut the door, and pray to your Father who is present in that secret place. Your Father who sees what you do in secret will reward you."*

It doesn't take a trip to Lourdes to experience love breaking through. There are many other ways to discover your own Holy Land. Weekly, I go to my favorite park in Nashville to experience God's presence. I also kneel and pray at the rustic altar in my own home. I read scripture and poetry. Spiritual wells are everywhere. Look for them. God is waiting to bless you with a little of heaven too.

---

* Matthew 6:6, CEB

Loving God,

If only I could begin again,
I would do things differently: Soul first.
I see now that everything is sacred.

Nothing would escape a "thank you,"
strangely, even the hard.
The reward is a strong, tender heart.

Be still, and listen, I would.
You are always whispering the Way.

I would be a poet of the ordinary,
revealing the extraordinary.

My tread would be oh so gentle on this Earth;
Peace, my middle name.

Ridiculous—marvelous,
the way I would love.

At every table,
I would give You the seat of honor.
And serve every kind of love.

I would radiate light—
even when the darkness courted my night and day.
Because Your hope does not disappoint.

It is a new day,
I will do things differently.
Soul first, I promise.

Amen.

Create an Altar in Your World

THE PURPOSE OF a pilgrimage is to connect with God in a new and deeper way. We don't have to travel to distant lands; we can commune with the Divine in our own homes. I love the idea of transforming ordinary spaces into mediators for grace. In medieval cathedrals, an altar was placed at the heart of the worship space. It was a "touchstone" where spiritual seekers could come for a hopeful encounter with God. Altars can be created anywhere.

Create an altar for yourself, somewhere in your day-to-day space that feels right, quiet, and somehow special. Start with a candle and a handwritten prayer. Then, day by day, week by week, lay items on the altar that give you hope and remind you of sacred things. Just passing by this small altar will give you a moment of peace and reflection in your heart. Maybe you include a bluebird feather found on a memorable walk in the woods, or a precious photo of your grandmother who loved you so well, or a thoughtful quote that draws you into a place of peace.

The objective is to create a space in your home that will trigger belief, peace, and hope. I have a table in my living room where I have placed my beloved statue of Mary, a votive in the shape of a star with a candle, an olive-wood cross that I can hold in my hand, a bud vase for a single stem, a tiny glass keepsake of holy water from my trip to Lourdes, and a book of prayers. Sometimes I sit by the table; other times I just glance at the altar from the corner of my eye, and I am reminded life is sacred.

22

Walk as if You Are Kissing the Earth with Your Feet

Many people are alive but don't touch the miracle of being alive.
—THICH NHAT HANH

The Lord bless you and keep you; the Lord make his face shine on you
and be gracious to you; the Lord turn his face toward you
and give you peace.
—NUMBERS 6:24–26 (NIV)

How does one kiss the earth with one's feet? If anyone could actually do that, it would probably be the gentle monk Thich Nhat Hanh,* who treaded softly in thought, word, and deed. I, on the other hand, pound the earth, heavy-footed, sometimes wearily dragging my humanity. Yet my spirit craves lightness of being. Peace. Thich Nhat Hanh says we should aim to live in such a way that we imprint peace and serenity on the Earth. A worthy goal.

In his book *Living Buddha, Living Christ,* Thich Nhat Hanh offers steps to live from a center of peace. He writes, "We do not have to die to arrive at the gates of Heaven. In fact, we have to be truly alive. The practice is to

---

* Thich Nhat Hanh was born October 11, 1926, in Vietnam and died January 22, 2022. He was exiled from his country for thirty-nine years because of his passionate pleas for peace during the Vietnam War. He studied at Princeton University, wrote over one hundred books, and founded the Plum Village, a monastery in the south of France. He was widely sought-after for his practice of mindful meditation. This monk led a walking meditation through the streets of New York City during a rush hour, proving inner peace is possible even in the midst of chaos.

touch life deeply so that the Kingdom of God becomes a reality. This is not a matter of devotion. It is a matter of practice. The Kingdom of God is available here and now."

We sometimes come close to peace, flirting with God and the spiritual reality, but we struggle to surrender completely and abide there all the time. I am more a spinning top than a kneeling monk. Still, Thich Nhat Hanh believed it is possible for all of us, even the frenetic ones, to experience the Kingdom here and now.

True peace is experienced as an interior quiet. A confidence. Regardless of exterior circumstances, all will be well. Nothing compares to this feeling of peace, love, and deep understanding in one's soul bones. As Thich Nhat Hanh proclaimed, "All is a miracle." One no longer needs power, control, or material success. One is at peace in all circumstances. This is a spiritual discipline; it takes intentional cultivation to embody tranquility in all life's circumstances. We have to believe God's promise in 2 Corinthians 12:9 (NIV), "My grace is sufficient for you." Only then, like Paul, can we be content in any circumstance and achieve peace.

The Zen Master dedicated his life to practicing inner peace, hoping it would spill out into the world. It takes practice and patience to cultivate calmness in the rush-hour ethos of our lives. Thich Nhat Hanh would ask: Are you in touch with the reality of God within you? He taught mindfulness to tap into the holy place of our souls. He begins by asking us to notice our breath and calmly, rhythmically surrender all human hang-ups. Thich Nhat Hanh instructs, "Breathing in, I know I am breathing in. Breathing out, I know I am breathing out." That is meditation in a nutshell! And it has the power to heal us.

I especially love the monk's "smile" meditation. It works! Every time you smile, hundreds of muscles relax in your body. Try it! Close your eyes. Take a calm, measured breath in through your nose. Hold it at the top for three seconds. Release your breath through your nose and smile. Watch what happens! You'll be amazed as the Benediction, "The Lord bless you and keep you; the Lord make his face shine on you and be gracious to you; the Lord turn his face toward you and give you peace,"* becomes more your day-to-day reality.

When we are able to stop, close our eyes, and focus on the breath, we find our lives are not as frenetic, heavy, or fragile as we once thought. Serenity does not happen overnight. With effort, peace can loosen the inner tangles. With each breath, each smile, we slowly learn to move with new lightness, kissing the earth with our feet.

Dear God,

Thank you for being the grounding of my being.
Wherever I go, whatever has been or will be,
on the most radiant days and dark-of-darkest nights,
You are there.
You call me by name.

Thank you for Your love,
it heals me from the inside out
and gives my life purpose.

Thank you for Your grace,
I miss the mark but You never give up on me,
instead offering another breath to try again.

Thank you for Your mysterious peace,

---

* Numbers 6:24–26, NIV

it covers my fear, my hurt, my doubt,
and blesses me with a lightness of being.

Thank you for Your hope,
no matter how difficult or despairing a situation,
You find a way.

Thank you for Your son,
He shows me the way of love.

Amen.

Tea Ceremony

I find few things more peaceful than enjoying a cup of tea. I adopted an English ritual in graduate school when I was living in London. Every day around 4:00 in the afternoon, following English custom, I would stop whatever I was doing and prepare a cup of tea with honey and a warmed chocolate chip cookie or ginger-snap. I would either sit in the heavily mullioned window of my tiny flat in the winter or out in my neighbor's serene Japanese garden. No work, no phone calls, no TV. Nothing happened in that fifteen-minute tea ceremony, except rest, reflection, laughter, and peace.

I can easily become more taskmaster than mystic, and that is a recipe for spiritual burnout. We all need more daily insertions of peace. It's less about the tea and more about stopping the spin and taking the time to recenter myself. The following is a recipe for a favorite tea, equally delicious hot or cold.

Ingredients

6 cups boiling water
2 herbal tea bags (hibiscus,
    rooibos, or chamomile citrus)
juice from 1 orange

juice from 1 lemon
2 tbsp organic honey
3 fresh sprigs mint

Directions

Combine hot water with tea bags in a teapot. Allow to steep for 6–8 minutes. Pour in your fresh orange and lemon juice, then honey, and garnish with fresh mint. Drink as is or add ice cubes for iced tea.

23

More Wonder!

Earth's crammed with heaven.
—ELIZABETH BARRETT BROWNING

No eye has seen, nor ear heard, nor the human heart conceived what
God has prepared for those who love [God].
—1 CORINTHIANS 2:9 (NRSV)

In the car on the way home from school each day, I ask the kids to recall a moment in their day when they experienced wonder—what we call that "fireworks on the inside" feeling! It could be anything—the taste of a warm chocolate chip cookie or spying a rainbow after a storm. You probably know it by the goose bumps on your arms. Or the way you can't help but smile at something. Or just the mysterious lift of your spirit.

Mystics define this experience as a brush with the Divine. A. W. Tozer captured it beautifully, saying, "When the eyes of the soul looking out meet the eyes of God looking in, heaven has begun right here on earth."

My kids live in a perpetual state of wonder, arms open to the world, exploring and embracing everything joyfully. Natural curiosity leads them to see, experience, and feel more. They are masters at spying the remarkable in the ordinary and taking their fill. No wonder Jesus instructs us to become like children to experience something of heaven.

Don't we all start out this way? Born wide-eyed and curious? No matter how distant it may feel, you still have a capacity for true awe. The relentless enemy of wonder is distraction. It can manifest in many ways, especially in a world that is constantly buzzing with noise and addicted to cramming our schedules with endless should-do's. In your life, distraction could be busyness, fatigue, anxiety—anything that keeps you from opening your eyes to glory in our midst.

Too hurried or jaded to see the marvelous? A hummingbird sighting, the smile of one's four-year-old, the first daffodil of spring, the table set with a delicious dinner and smiling faces—these are gifts that animate our souls if we allow them to. The poet John O'Donohue wrote, "Every life is braided with luminous moments." My honeybees are a marvel to me. They will travel miles for the reward of nectar. Our souls are nourished on experiences of awe, where the ordinary reveals itself to be anything but. Perspectives shift, as well as our capacity to hope, when we wake up to the fact that we are participants in a world of incomparable beauty, infinite mystery, and humbling sanctity. Divinity permeates everything.

Despite our culture's obsession with bullying and breaking hearts, the truth is our world is filled with unimaginable goodness and beauty, to be found even in moments of trial. Jesus gives simple instructions: "Consider the lilies of the field . . . they neither toil nor spin, and . . . even Solomon in all his glory, was not arrayed like one of these."* The poet Emily Dickinson confessed, "Consider the lilies of the field" was the only commandment she never broke.

Finding wonder in the smallest things became a spiritual discipline (and survival skill) during my son's cancer. We spent six to eight high-stress hours at the hospital every day for a year. I made a silent pact that I would do one thing a day that gave me joy and kept me hopeful.

The world does not lack for wonder. **Your ordinary, everyday life is a field of buried treasure.**

---

* Matthew 6:28–29, NKJV

God,

You stitched a map of heaven into the pocket of my soul,
so I would never be completely lost from You.
Entrusted me with a short but important mission
in the realm of Earth,
a rite of passage for my incomparable soul.

Will I realize my celestial powers in time—
get to the sacred thick of it?
Or will I become distracted
and miss the Divine point?

I had no idea how challenging the journey would be,
and how marvelously sacred.
Sometimes the cosmic teachers
of pain, loss, and doubt shift my attention.

Help me to embrace the immensity of the experience—
the beauty, the mysteries, the heaven breakthroughs.
Become a collector of grace.
One day I will show up at heaven's door, and with me,
a heart brimming with wonder.
More time, please!

Amen.

What Delights You?

OUR CULTURE HAS slipped into a terrible habit of filling free, empty moments with "screen scrolling" to nowhere. Studies have found that we do experience a release of dopamine (the happy hormone) in our brains with every swipe. But the delight is fleeting when compared to our spirit's response to catching a rainbow after a storm, the taste of a warm banana chocolate chip muffin, or receiving a hug. Scrolling through your Instagram reel is cotton candy for your spirit. We falsely believe this distraction relieves stress or adds something of value to our lives. Instead, we are left with nothing to show for our time except increased anxiousness and insecurity.

Commit to one week of no social media. State on your feed that you are taking a break. It will encourage others to do the same (maybe even try this exercise with a friend if you would benefit from the accountability). Fill the time with activities that nurture your soul. Take a walk. Set up a bird feeder outside your window. Call your funniest friend for a laugh. Clip some flowers from your garden, arrange them in a mason jar, and gift it to your neighbor. Relish a warm chocolate chip cookie and a cup of tea. Watch how much more peaceful you will become.

During this week, keep a daily mental or physical list of delights you discover, whether new or familiar. Text them to your partner, put them on sticky notes on your mirror, write them on your grocery list—just find a way to remember and celebrate experiences of wonder and simple joy. Then, model your commitment to real life over screen time. Around the dinner table, share fireworks moments from your day that fed your soul.

24

Who Takes the Lead?

Walk now, into whatever comes next, knowing that God
who is love, is always, always walking with you.
—TALLU SCHUYLER QUINN

Teach me to do Your will, For You are my God;
Let Your good Spirit lead me on level ground.
—PSALM 143:10 (NASB)

We have a menagerie of animals at our house, almost a Noah's
Ark–ful! Our most recent addition is a brother-and-sister pair of
huskies. I confess . . . it was a result of Christmas parental weakness. Who
wouldn't want a couple of cute puppies under the tree? What were we
thinking? It didn't take long before I discovered that huskies have a lot of
energy and constantly leap and bound. On many afternoons, the kids and
I will take them for a long trek around the neighborhood. Each time, inevitably, one husky pulls forward and takes the lead.

This a good metaphor for how we humans navigate in the world.

In any given moment, significant or mundane, it could be our demanding ego or generous soul that takes the lead. In my quest to live a humble
life, I regularly have to check myself, since the world is ever rewarding
egoic performance. More often than I would like to admit, my ego slyly
slips into the lead. A lot of good things are missed when I allow this to
happen. People are overlooked. I feel shallow. But when I approach the
world from my more gentle and vulnerable side, I access the divine in me,

and that experience is exponentially different. Suddenly, I view the world through the eyes of God, and my life becomes a canvas brimming with possibilities to impact others for good.

David Brooks, in his illuminating book *The Second Mountain: The Quest for a Moral Life*, sets up a two-mountain metaphor to help us distinguish whether we are leading an ego-driven or soul-directed life. He says you should know which mountain you are climbing by the measure of your inner joy.

The ego leads a mountain climb geared toward achievement, recognition, and acquisition. We build careers, reputations, and financial security on this mountain. We measure our value through the eyes of others. Society tells us this mountain is *the* mountain, and it cheers our rise. Many summit this mountain and are uninspired by the view. They yearn for something more.

The soul chooses a different ascent. One focused on the quality of relationships, the ability to maintain inner peace, having a keen eye for the wondrous, and a willingness to lose the ego in pursuit of a much better goal. On this mountain, expect moments of transcendence, being stunned by beauty and the profundity of love's capacity. One intuits there is something larger than self at work here, love-bent and redemptive, and pursues it with gusto.

Eighteen years ago, I was eagerly hiking the switchbacks up the first mountain, believing I was "living the life." Then a pediatric oncologist shoved me off a cliff with the words "Your child has stage 4 cancer." Suddenly, what I thought was important and meaningful turned to ash right before my eyes. This near tragedy was a soul opener, affording me the opportunity to choose the second mountain and to live a deeper, more meaningful life.

I wish I could tell you that I have remained on that second mountain, that I experienced my own Damascus Road epiphany, never looking back. The truth is, there are days and seasons that I find myself right back on the tempting, well-traveled path of the first mountain, my ego leading the charge. Sometimes the earthly wins feel too good to resist, but they never seem to last or satisfy my needs. An interior tug-of-war is part of the spiritual journey. What I find is that I tire easily, even burn out, when my ego is in charge. Body, mind, and soul, I crave a spiritual reset.

If you are wondering which mountain you are climbing, ask yourself where you spend the bulk of your time, talent, and treasure. Look around—do the people who cross your path know you by your outpoured love or your success? Is gratitude a guiding emotion in your daily life? The reality is we are all going to get tripped up by our egos and have less-than-stellar days. Too easily, pride can eclipse the purest part of ourselves. But God is focused on what we will do next, always giving us chances to curb the ego and live from the best in us.

We are standing at the trailhead; which mountain is it to be today? May your soul take the lead!

Merciful God,

Today I took my soul out for a walk.
She moved oh-so-slowly,
not to miss a petal, a love whisper, a quiet touch.
She talked to the trees, smiled at the grocery clerk,
brought common ground into every encounter.

A child again,
eager and full of wonder,
she bestowed words of encouragement,

hearts lifted at her passing,
her hope, contagious.

You won't catch her chasing status
or overstocking her barns.
These leave her feeling empty and wanting more.
Instead she takes her fill of beauty and grace.

Following her intuition
(why not use a superpower if you have one, right?),
she is drawn deep beneath the surface of things,
where the Gospel lives.

She closes the day humble, satiated with love,
her countenance glowing with gratitude.

Why do I not take my soul out every day?

Amen.

Matcha Latte

On my daily walks with the huskies, I often need a jump start. I must admit that I have never been a fan of green tea. It has always tasted like wet dog to me! But matcha is different. It is the actual green-tea leaves ground up into a potent powder. A cup of matcha is an excellent source of antioxidants, boosts the immune system, and is great for the skin. And unlike coffee, which makes your heart race and your hands shake, the caffeine found in green tea promotes a calm alertness in the brain. Zen Buddhist monks have used green tea for well over a millennium to enhance their practice of meditation. Matcha contains the amino acid L-theanine, which elevates the production of dopamine and serotonin; both are proven to elevate the mood, improve memory, and increase concentration.

Join me in making a delicious and healthy matcha latte and set out on a slow, purposeful walk, meditating on which part of yourself (ego or generous soul) you will allow to take the lead this week.

Happy trails!

Ingredients

1 tsp matcha powder
¼ cup boiling water
1 cup almond or coconut milk

1 tsp wildflower honey
turmeric, for garnish
cinnamon, for garnish

Directions

For this matcha latte, I use 1 teaspoon of matcha powder. I pour ¼ cup of hot water over the green powder, then stir the mixture with a bamboo whisk. Second, I use my Nescafé milk frother, heat up a cup of almond milk, and pour it over the green liquid. Stir in honey and sprinkle the top with turmeric and cinnamon, and it feels like you are drinking a luxuriant dessert.

25

It's an Inside Job

Promise me you'll always remember: You are braver than you
believe, and stronger than you seem, and smarter than you think.
—A. A. MILNE

Do you not know that you are God's temple
and that God's Spirit dwells in you?
—1 CORINTHIANS 3:16 (NRSV)

Some years ago, my family made a weekend road trip to South Carolina to visit my extended family. The Suburban was packed full with six kids, our golden retriever, many little bags of goldfish crackers, a case of juice boxes, two large sacks of peanut M&Ms, eight sub sandwiches, lots of crayons and coloring books, jellybeans galore, school bookbags, special pillows, and stuffed animals.

When we returned home to Nashville, the car looked like a tornado had swirled through it. Gooey chocolate smears, sticky apple juice stains, crushed goldfish crackers in every nook and cranny, pacifiers jammed between the seats, broken and melted crayons, all surrounded by the very unpleasant scent of wet dog. Surprisingly, the outside of the car looked gloriously brand-new. The inside—a masterpiece of disaster.

My sister took one look at the interior and suggested Stephen's mobile car-cleaning company, whose slogan is "I've seen everything!" When Stephen arrived, he inspected the state of the vehicle. His look was grave, and after an uncomfortable silence, I sheepishly asked him, "What is it going to take?"

He scratched his head before replying, "I can put a polish on those outside scratches and she'll look even better than new. But, ma'am, what you really need is a total inside job!"

It got me thinking. Does the exterior of my life reflect what's truly happening on the inside of me?

So often, we present to the world a picture that is polished and near perfection, but inside we are hot messes. Instead of finding M&Ms and spilled apple juice, as was inside my Suburban, one look inside our souls and we find insecurity, jealousy, and fear. Open the heart compartment and we find hurt and disappointment. Lift the floor mat of the mind and discover impatience, envy, and selfishness. We all have interior spaces that could use a tidying in order to operate more lovingly and honorably.

I confess, my inside self can look much like the interior of my old Suburban. I am my own tornado, juggling all the roles I play in my life. I may appear serenely in charge on the outside, but often I am frantic on the inside. It is in these moments that I need to take a breath, let go of my unrealistic expectations, and drop some responsibilities. We must stop buying into the idea of "more is better" and embrace "sacred is best."

An inside job requires discipline and effort. Therapy, either professional, ministerial, or with a family member or trusted friend, is necessary for working through our interior tangles and healing wounds. Commit to practices that encourage a healthy mind, body, and spirit: exercise, sleep, good nutrition, and meditation. Invest in a community of people who support and celebrate one's effort to be whole inside and out. Deepen your spiritual life with prayer, worship, books, soulfull podcasts, and quiet reflection. Balance will come, and freedom will follow.

Create a life that feels good on the inside, not one that just looks good on the outside.

Divine One,

*What would You discover if You gazed inside to
the anatomy of my soul?*

*Would You see a noble spirit,
one that is drawn to hope,
peaceful and not afraid of Your mystery?*

*Would I be full of faith, trusting in You for my today
and tomorrow?*

*Would you feel gentleness and a depth of compassion,
delighting in the corners of my soul, where I have set aside
my ego
and given wholly over to the needs of another?*

*Would You hear words of kindness and mercy spoken
from me?*

*Would I radiate a special kind of light,
one with the power to cut through the darkness?*

You know me from the inside out.

*The truth is I am vulnerable.
I hurt.
I doubt.
I hope.*

I yearn for healing and wholeness.
I need You.

Amen.

Honor the Sabbath

TWENTY-FIVE YEARS AGO, I shared an office in New York with an Orthodox Jewish couple who truly honored the commandment to observe the Sabbath, which is a day set aside each week for rest and reflection. Thursday evenings were spent cooking and cleaning their apartment in preparation for Shabbat. From dusk on Friday until dusk on Saturday, they were forbidden to do any work. My friend, Sarah, equated the spiritual practice to a weekly vacation. She and her husband would listen to music, read books, nap, take a walk in the park, make love. I remember thinking this was a tad indulgent. Another colleague commented, "Look at the time they lose!"

How wrong and naive we were! Sabbath is God's gift to us. It is a healing balm for our task-obsessed, achievement-focused, worn-out culture. The spiritual discipline is an invitation to address the interior of our "Suburbans" so we can move through the world with more peace and joy.

Sabbath-keeping is an invitation to let go of "the work" of being human: the fears, the responsibilities, the constant ticking of the clock—so that we breathe, heal, remember that we are holy creatures. We need time for renewal: to dream, clarify, and explore our relationship with the Divine.

God has given us permission to simply let go. The reality is our souls need time off the clock! Give yourself permission to cease working altogether. It's called soul care!

The objective is to embrace the needs of your soul and nurture them. I work on Sunday mornings, but Sunday afternoons entail pajamas, sitting in the garden with a cup of tea, and opening a new novel for the pure pleasure of it. This week, pick a day (Sundays are most practical for me), forgo the work of being human, and honor whatever delights you.

If you are stumped on how to Sabbath: Do what delights! You can

worship,
cook,
garden,
pray,
practice downward dog,
read,
play the piano,
listen to a sonata,
dance,
or cuddle with a loved one.

26

Not Another PB&J

The soul is not a mechanical problem to be solved;
it's a living being that has to be fed.
—THOMAS MOORE

Everything is possible for one who believes.
—MARK 9:23 (NIV)

M any years ago, a wise friend shared an anecdote to help me positively embrace a new chapter in my life and have the courage to
make a change.

In the story, a lunch bell rings at noon every day on a construction site.
Hammers and nails are exchanged for lunch pails and thermoses. Laughing and cajoling, workmates sit down together on the newly finished re-
taining wall to partake of their midday meal.

"Not another peanut butter and jelly sandwich," the foreman, Joe,
complains as he opens the wax-paper-enfolded sandwich.

"I hate peanut butter and jelly," he bemoans, eyeing his co-laborers'
tastier selections.

Day after day, week after week, the bell rings, the crew gathers for
lunch, and the foreman opens up his pail to find another peanut butter
and jelly sandwich.

"It's peanut butter and jelly again, daggonit!"

Finally, an exasperated pal barks, "Why don't you just tell your wife to fix you something else? Tell her you don't like peanut butter and jelly sandwiches and be done with it. Try a meatball sub."

"What wife?" he says with annoyance. "I ain't married. I make my own sandwich every day."

There are circumstances in our lives that we have absolutely no control over. But there are a lot that we do control. If we were to make an honest inspection of our lives, from our personal relationships to the quality of our health to our soul's well-being, we would see many missed opportunities. Every day we get to make our own metaphorical sandwiches. In the grand design of this glory project called Life, our free will is a self-destructor or remarkable launcher. We are the CEOs of our unique destinies. Our daily choices can stop us in place, even set us up for defeat. Or guide us into an evolving and love-directed fullness of life.

We desire perfect choices, painless happiness, and complete understanding. Because there are no probabilities that we will ever get these, we can slip into what I call the peanut-butter-and-jelly rut. We repeat patterns that rob us of meaningful lives. We hold on with a vise grip to past hurts and growth-averse perspectives. We participate in relationships that diminish us and others. We allow fear to cancel our hope. We invest in the culture of the day, instead of the desire of our eternal souls. Days turn into years. We stop bearing new fruit.

The peanut-butter-and-jelly rut sucks the possibility of real joy, and the potential for new opportunities, out of our lives. I have made many peanut-butter-and-jelly choices in my time, where I either played it safe or operated from fear, knowing there were other paths and then feeling remorse for my lack of creativity, even cowardice.

What if we woke up tomorrow and, instead of making the same old peanut butter and jelly sandwich, decided to try a tartine? Have the courage to step out of one's comfort zone, ignore ego pride, and embrace a new outlook, a new path.

This week, acknowledge what is truly needed in your marriage, family, workplace, and friendships. Then, take ownership of a new role in them. Honor your body as a gift, not to be taken for granted, ignored, or mistreated. Laugh! Take off your shoes and feel the grass under your feet and the sun on your face. Soulfull living begins with an awareness of your thought patterns and a commitment, with God's help, to rightly respond to them. Leave the tired, old ways of thinking at home. Dare to evolve. Aim for growth in every area of your life, from your relationships to your personal faith. Do at least one soulfull activity a day. We control how we step forward into our daily destiny.

Today is not going to be a peanut-butter-and-jelly-sandwich day for me! How about you?

Beloved,

Today I pray for a triumph.
A daffodil to push up from the cold earth.
A moment where courage surprises
and I win a round.
Goodness steals the spotlight from despair.
The impossible is
made marvelously possible.
You shine brighter than the tragic.
Hope taps me on the shoulder,
and together we walk into the sun

making great plans.
My soul no longer plays the understudy
but takes center stage.
I fall in love with life;
life falls in love with me.
Heaven is not a mirage
but an oasis within me.

Amen.

Tartines

Today why not choose to forgo peanut butter and jelly for a delicious French tartine? Visit any quaint neighborhood bistro or a café in France in the summer, and you are sure to find *tartine du jour* on the menu. This popular open-faced sandwich is the French creative take on fast food. Leave it to the French to take a slice of rustic sourdough, dress it with interesting and colorful toppings, and voilà! You have something effortlessly elegant on the plate! The tartine provides a fragrant and colorful canvas of fresh ingredients—a cornucopia of nuts, cheeses, fruits, vegetables, and cured meats drizzled with honey, olive oil, and balsamic vinegar. Invite a friend over for lunch! Bon appétit!

Ingredients

sliced peaches, toasted hazelnuts, ricotta cheese, basil, and a drizzle of honey

cherries, pistachios, and Manchego cheese

avocado, Parmesan ribbons, a squeeze of lemon, and a sprinkle of fleur de sel

heirloom tomatoes, pesto, and creamy buffalo mozzarella

sliced pears, prosciutto, Parmesan ribbons, and a balsamic glaze

shaved radishes, slathered with French salted butter and adorned with fresh dill

sliced figs, toasted walnuts, Roquefort cheese, and rosemary honey

smoked salmon, crème fraîche, a bouquet of dill, and a squeeze of lemon

flank steak, arugula, and Parmesan ribbons

fresh-ground almond butter and Nutella

roasted vegetables, pesto, and ribbons of pecorino cheese

Directions

Choose a hearty loaf of bread or French baguette and slice thickly. Drizzle slices with olive oil or—my favorite—spread with salted Irish butter. Toast the bread under the broiler, then layer with colorful ingredients (see above for suggestions of combinations). Accompany the open-faced sandwiches with a green salad and light vinaigrette, a cup of gazpacho or chilled-cucumber yogurt mint soup, and a glass of rosé, and voilà, you have a memorable meal!

27

Lions, Tigers, Bears, Oh My!

Hope reflects the state of your soul rather than the circumstances
surrounding your days.
—WILLIAM SLOANE COFFIN

For I know the plans I have for you . . . plans to prosper you and not to
harm you, plans to give you hope and a future.
—JEREMIAH 29:11 (NIV)

One recent summer, I had a fearsome encounter with a bear—but not an ordinary bear! She was the Grand Matriarch of the Tetons, decked out in her shaggy fur coat, with four yearlings in tow. A magnificent creature, and absolutely terrifying—she weighed four hundred pounds and stood seven feet tall. In Grand Teton National Park, she is listed as Grizzly 399, but everyone knows this lady as the most famous grizzly bear in the world. She has her own Facebook, Twitter, and Instagram accounts, and several books have been written about her.

Do you know how dangerous a grizzly mother bear is, especially if you come between her and her cubs? Google "bear attacks" to know why that day my heart was in my throat and fight-or-flight adrenaline coursed through my veins.

"Lions and tigers and bears—oh my. Lions and tigers and bears—oh my. Lions and tigers and bears—oh my." The Wizard of Oz was a childhood favorite. Who could forget Dorothy, Scarecrow, and the Tin Man, paralyzed in

fear, singing the "Lions and tigers and bears" fear-chant on the Yellow Brick Road? That day in Grand Teton National Park, I wanted to shout it.

When I got the call from my dear friend Tallu with her devastating glioblastoma diagnosis, when a line of tornadoes destroyed miles of Tennessee, when my dad got a serious case of COVID-19, each time I experienced that same grizzly-bear fear. It's a familiar tune on most Friday nights, waiting for my teenagers to come home. *Lions and tigers and bears—oh my!*

I confess—sometimes reality can really scare me. I'm so heart-invested in my own life, this beautiful old world, and the people I love in it. I am terrified to lose any sacred piece of it.

I had grizzly-bear, Yellow-Brick-Road panic attacks for over a year during my son's treatments for cancer. I'll never forget the day Charlie's oncologist at Memorial Sloan Kettering leaned across his desk and stopped me midsentence in my list of what-ifs: *What if the chemo stunts his growth? What if the chemo kills brain cells and he has limited intelligence? What if the chemo doesn't work? What if the cancer comes back?* Abruptly, and almost angrily, he said, "Farrell, fear will not save your son. Flipping through the Rolodex of what-ifs is a waste of your time and mine too. It will get us nowhere. Focus your energy on all the possibilities of healing. Charlie doesn't need your fear. He needs your hope."

However humbling to hear, that moment with Dr. K was a game changer for me and will be for the rest of my life. But there are days when I still get triggered. Sometimes my list of fears is longer than my list of hopes. On my better days, I counter the internal fear-rant with a cosmos rally: "Dear God, Be with me. Just be with me now." This is my own "Yellow Brick Road" song of hope.

My friend Kate Wilmot is the bear-management specialist at Grand

Teton National Park. I called her immediately after the summer's epic run-in with Grizzly 399. She told me that black bears and dangerous grizzlies are everywhere, but that should never discourage one from trailblazing. Usually, they show up when we least expect them, so just be prepared. Travel in a group and carry your bear spray. If you come upon a real or metaphorical bear, whatever you do, don't panic. Bad things happen when you scream or run. Pull your group together so you look big and tall in the face of the bear. Respond in the moment with a calm, nonanxious presence. Wait patiently. The bear will move on. Her bear-safety wisdom is applicable to my day-to-day life.

Did you know that only *two* fatal bear attacks happen in North America annually? So much real estate in our hearts is given to fears that actually never amount to anything! I always return to this Psalmist's confession: "Yea, though I walk through the valley of the shadow of death, I will fear no evil: for thou art with me."* The Psalmist knew there would be plenty of lions, tigers, and bears on our Yellow Brick Roads. But in trusting God, he pressed onward for the reward of a rich and meaningful life.

No matter how strong your faith armor or how pleasant your current Yellow Brick trek, fear will come for you, aiming to pierce your heart. For this reason, God proclaimed, "Do not be afraid," 365 times in the Bible. Have faith that God created us to do brave things. And remember, "Be with me," and "Help!" are worthy prayers; don't be afraid to pray them—often!

---

* Psalm 23:4, KJV

A "Hope Chant" Prayer
on Any Yellow Brick Road

God has me, whatever happens.
God is with me and invested in my outcome.
God will put people in my path to help me.
No matter how devastating the winter,
my spring will come.
Hope is real and will not disappoint.
Healing is daily possible.
My soul is eternal and will live on.

Temper the Fear

THIS WEEK, SEE if you can meet the uncertainty and fear in your life with a renewed trust in God. As you brave your Yellow Brick Road, use these truths and actionable items to make your way forward.

1. Speak your fears. The moment you share the burden, it loses power over you.

2. Commit to the discipline of prayer, breathing exercises, and meditation. Your first defense when the fear-chant erupts is not to panic, but to be calm.

3. We are going to encounter real and metaphorical bears. There is no avoiding them, so find your Scarecrow, your Tin Man, and your

Lion—family and friends of faith. God gave us each other for a reason.

4. Regular physical exercise eases the fight-or-flight reflex.

5. Put away the Rolodex of what-ifs, and focus on what can be managed right in front of you.

28

Keep Casting!

When you do things from your soul, you feel a river
moving in you, a joy.
—RUMI

Ask and it will be given to you; seek and you will find;
knock and the door will be opened to you.
—MATTHEW 7:7 (NIV)

The summer after my sophomore year of college at Sewanee, I boarded a plane and headed west for the first time. My heart had fallen for a certain green-eyed angler who spent his mornings working construction in Teton Village, Wyoming, and his afternoons casting dry flies for trout on the challenging Snake River. Twenty-five years later, I remain entranced by the graceful *pas de deux* of my noble young angler, now husband, and his beloved river.

A fly fisherman gently laying his line upon the fast-changing countenance of the river is reminiscent of a Zen master flowing through his daily meditation. Each is in search of something—a catch, a connection, a gift of peace, a glimpse of goodness, a deeper experience of reality. A seasoned angler like my husband recognizes that something remarkable, even transcendent, can happen anytime the line is cast into the current. He approaches the river and life with reverence and a peaceful posture. No wonder he is called the fish whisperer in our family.

Sometimes in life we are gifted with a tug on an invisible line, delicately hooking our very souls. In this moment, we are poignantly aware and grateful that we are connected to something otherworldly and greater than ourselves. Despite all the tangled lines, the unpredictable clouds, and the disappointing days when we come up empty-handed, we know our lives have divine significance. It's what keeps drawing us back to the river, and life.

Keep casting into the river, angling for meaning, and being enchanted by the whole experience. Some days we have to venture past the comfortable bank to catch a fish, or, in life, to experience a glimmer of God. There will be days, maybe many, when we will leave the metaphorical river skunked. But if love is our guide, eventually we will land a fish, and in the process our lives will find their true meaning. My daily prayer always is for more time to cast my line. Nothing compares to that tug on the soul: an experience of heaven on Earth.

Following are some lessons from the river to encourage a deeper, more fulfilled human spiritual experience.

Lesson 1

Recognize that in every moment, something sacred could be on the line. A fish, a dream, a relationship, an experience of God. It can be hooked or lost forever. Pay attention. Ask, seek, knock.

Lesson 2

God is not concerned with the number of scriptures you can quote, the length of your downward dog in yoga, the number of minutes you meditate, or your perfect attendance at chapel. The spiritual life is intimate and begs authenticity only. Believe that when you pray, the Beloved is listening. Know that God is present when you catch the spectacular rainbow trout *and* when you leave the river with an empty pail. Discovering the divinity within and all around you is a lifelong adventure.

Lesson 3

Be curious. Avid fishermen are always in search of "honey holes" on the river where there is a greater chance for a catch. Put yourself in places where God is likely to show up. Observe nature, participate in a spiritual community, light a candle and pray, practice yoga, extend kindness to those in need, and be open to new relationships and experiences that encourage a holier existence.

Lesson 4

Surround yourself with friends and family who do not diminish your spirit but rather champion it. Do not be so hard on yourself and others. Realize we are all trying to catch the glory the best way we can.

Lesson 5

All anglers know that storms come out of nowhere. One moment it's all sunshine and smiles; the next we are faced with unmerciful weather and frightened to our core by the crackle of lightning. Adapt to circumstances. Remember, like the river flows, God is moving each of us forward in the direction of wholeness.

Dear God,

The River of Life is a winding mystery,
shimmering with possibility.
With your help, I will keep angling for grace,
increasing goodness on my side of the bank,
searching for silver linings in the pain,
waiting faithfully for joy to tip the balance of sorrow,
holding on to hope in the dark, and
making sacrifices for the Good.
The story of the river is one of love.
May my life be meaningful in your beautiful tale.
Let me live to cast my line for another day.

Amen.

Poisson en Papillote (Fish)

I'm pulling out all the fancy French words! *Poisson en papillote* simply means "fish cooked in parchment"! It is so easy and flavorful, and did I mention easy? It is also a healthy, quick way to steam your just-caught fish and a mélange of vegetables. Because I am married to an angler, fish is often on the menu. I discovered this recipe fifteen years ago in a French cookbook, but feel free to be creative and spontaneous with what you include in your culinary envelope. The beauty of this recipe is you can prepare a foil packet for each person joining your table for dinner. It makes for a fun dinner and easy cleanup!

Ingredients

6 fillets white fish of your choosing
    (trout, cod, sea bass, tilapia)
olive oil
herbes de Provence
Maldon or kosher salt
fresh-ground pepper
2-3 tomatoes, diced and seeded

2 cups Mediterranean olives
6 sprigs fresh thyme
1 zucchini
1 eggplant
1 squash
1 red onion

Directions

Preheat oven to 350°F. Cut six 12-inch squares of parchment or foil, one for each fillet. I have prepared this recipe using sea bass, but I am sure it would be just as delicious with any other mild, white poisson (fish)! Place a fillet of fish in the center of the parchment, drizzle olive oil all over it, sprinkle herbes de Provence evenly over the fish (don't go overboard with dried herbs, because fish is more delicate than chicken), as well as salt and pepper. Each foil packet is gifted with a handful of diced tomatoes, olives, and one sprig of fresh thyme. Bring up the edges of the parchment, crease sides together, fold, and seal tightly. Place all the packets together on a baking sheet. Bake until the fish is opaque. I would check after 15 minutes.

Create another packet for your vegetables, including zucchini, remaining tomato, eggplant, squash, onion, and olives. Prepare the vegetables the same way you did the fish: a generous coating of olive oil, herbes de Provence, salt, pepper, and a sprig or two of fresh thyme. The vegetables might need 15–20 minutes—they are better al dente. Slice up a French baguette for the table and enjoy your catch!

29
The Journey of the Soul

Let nothing disturb you.
Let nothing frighten you.
All things are passing away:
God never changes.
Patience obtains all things.
Whoever has God lacks nothing;
God alone suffices.
—ST. TERESA D'AVILA

For we know that if the earthly tent we live in is destroyed,
we have a building from God, an eternal house in heaven . . .
Now the one who has fashioned us for this very purpose is God,
who has given us the Spirit as a deposit, guaranteeing what is to come.
Therefore we are always confident.
—2 CORINTHIANS 5:1, 5–6 (NIV)

I participate in enough funerals to know that everyone, including me, is hoping that at our end, the lights will dim, a big screen will lower, and God will play the movie trailer for Eternity. What excitement and total relief it would be to get a peek at the next chapter in the life of our souls.

The poet Emily Dickinson articulates her desired fate in "Poem 479":

*Because I could not stop for Death—He kindly
stopped for me—The Carriage held but just
Ourselves—And Immortality.*

Dickinson, like myself, believed in an ultimate hope. That doesn't mean that I do not struggle with endings. Death is scary, and the loss of anyone with whom there was an authentic exchange of love is wretched. In my ministry role, I have gratefully witnessed a mystical peace tenderly embracing a departing spirit. I am convinced angels are waiting in the eaves to show the way. It's those of us left behind, the mourners, who suffer the greatest. Not only does loss make us fear our own end, but it's a sucker-punch hurt like nothing else we experience on Earth.

Even the most steadfast of us fight tooth and nail to keep the faith in the face of deep loss. Grief is strange and unnatural, but a universal reality. The best way I can describe grief is that suddenly and without your permission, you ingest a foreign object not meant for your body to digest but with no way to vacate it. It takes up residence in your secret inner being. That foreign body travels through you unmercifully, with no real direction or destination. Every movement is an interior lashing on the tender parts of you, leaving invisible bruises and terrible emptiness. Someone integral to who you are and how you find your being in the world has been taken away. You find yourself grateful for grief's torment because it means that person is still part of you. Other times you are so angry you'd like to turn your back on God. You think, *No one should hurt like this.*

Some say grief is the price of love. Even if it's true, the sentiment is not an easy healing balm. The loss never leaves us, but it softens enough, with the help of grace, so that we can find again the coordinates of joy. Jesus says, "Blessed are those who mourn, for they will be comforted."* I believe God is especially close to the brokenhearted.

There is no cure for mortality, but I lean into Jesus as a model for how to reconcile the fear, the grief, the doubt, and faithfully surrender.

---

* Matthew 5:4, NIV

I imagine in the quiet of the Garden of Gethsemane, Jesus spent some time remembering the people and experiences that had blessed his life with meaning and joy. I bet he also made a mental list of all the things he would miss terribly when he was gone. No more springs in Jerusalem, with all the blooming almond trees. Or gatherings around a big table spilling with his family and friends, good food and wine, stories and laughter. No more music, dancing, embraces, kisses, or hearing the words "I love you."

Jesus knew that to be human is an exquisite experience.

In the secret places of my heart and yours, we have to decide to trust God. To trust in the Divine plan that has been in motion for billions of years, one that reveals God's miraculous intention of resurrection and new life. To trust in an infinite Love to carry us and our loved ones through the end of what we know, to enter a marvelous, divine "next."

We mourn together for all that we love and lose while here on Earth. We are grateful that one day there will be an end to all suffering. We place our hope in Eternity.

Beloved,

You measure life in infinitudes.
Birth and death are not the bookends
for the story of the soul.
My spirit is not bound by time and space.
There are no true goodbyes.

Grief is the result of loving well.
One day I will face a particular end,
but never The End.

To live in hope—finally—
is to live abundantly here and now,
to meet death not as the finale,
but a mysterious door
that, once I step through,
begins the next adventure.

Amen.

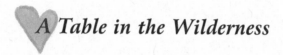 *A Table in the Wilderness*

I HAVE MY friend Tallu to thank for gifting me with the phrase "a table in the wilderness." It has since become my personal code word for manifesting hope. In his lowest moment of uncertainty, fear, and grief, Jesus set up a table, invited his closest friends, and then fed them hope.

When grief strikes, the natural inclination is to retreat into a dark cave. Sometimes I believe we have to force hope's hand by metaphorically setting up a table in our wilderness. It could be the simplest gesture of putting a handful of sunflowers in a bud vase by the kitchen sink. Or playing a song on repeat that has lifted our spirits in the past. Maybe it's calling our funniest friend for a needed laugh. Maybe we set "a table in the wilderness" by planning a future trip to the beach or mountains, printing out pictures of the place, and taping them to the refrigerator door. We schedule appointments months out with our counselor for cry sessions. We force ourselves to get out of our pajamas, dress slap-dash, and take a walk in nature. We do the opposite of what we feel and accept the invitation to join friends for dinner. We open the Bible to the Psalms and allow the words to be a soul balm and roadmap forward.

Each of us is going to experience grief and watch those we love grieve. God wants us to find our joy again. In the words of the Psalmist, "weeping may linger for the night, but joy comes with the morning."* Let "Set a table in the wilderness" be your code for meeting grief with hope. Help others do the same.

---

* Psalm 30:5, NRSV

30

Hope Does Not Disappoint

It's much more radical, much more daring,
and much more dangerous to hope.
—MARY KARR

Those who hope in the Lord will renew their strength. They will soar
on wings like eagles; they will run and not grow weary.
—ISAIAH 40:31 (NIV)

I have an intuitive gift—my family would call it a terrible habit—of fig-
uring out the plot and then announcing in the middle of a story, "I know
how this one is going to end!" But I confess—the story God is writing with
our lives consistently leaves me stumped. Sometimes it makes no logical
sense. It feels awfully unjust. Paul's conclusion in 1 Corinthians 13:12, "We
see in a mirror dimly,"* feels like a cosmic slap in the face. When my friend
Isse died of colon cancer at the age of forty-five, leaving three precious children and her soulmate behind, I called out to the cosmos like an angry
fishwife, "How could you let the heroine die halfway through her story?"

Corrie ten Boom, in her powerful memoir *The Hiding Place*, wrote,
"When a train goes through a tunnel and it gets dark, you don't throw
away the ticket and jump off. You sit still and trust the engineer." The
exact trajectory of our lives remains a mystery to everyone—except for
God. I believe God gives us a "big picture" outline, and even hints to how

---

* NASB

our story will end. But we should count on some dark tunnels to go through where we'll wonder if the light will ever find us again.

To believe in hope, sometimes we need more than just words. Like the disciple Thomas, we would like to see physical proof of hope with our own eyes. We can lean on science—astrophysics, actually—for a bit of tangible proof of an eternal hope.

God loves stars. I have counted well over one hundred celestial references in the Bible. Not only does God use them—like the Christmas Star, for example, to show us the way to love in a manger in Bethlehem—but God also creates us to be stars, with our own unique charge of light. Science can now back that up. Carl Sagan, the renowned astrophysicist and astronomer, proclaimed, "We are made of star-stuff." Just like Polaris and the billions of constellations in the Milky Way, we are a living composite of oxygen, carbon, iron, nickel, and a myriad of other celestial elements. We are designed to shine.

It's the life pattern of a star that is most compelling to the hope hypothesis. Once a star has accomplished its mission in the universe and has used up all its energy, it explodes as a supernova and sheds all its layers. The star is transformed. What's left behind is the core of the star, known as the neutron star. And scientists have proved that the core will glow for hundreds of billions of years. Eternity. Just as God promises in the scriptures, anything made in love will have no end.

The earthly experience is never going to be perfect or pain-free. When there appears no light at the end of the tunnel, look around; often *we* are the light *in* the tunnel for one another. Have faith, God is working within every circumstance and person for redemption.

Hope is the litmus test for the state of my soul and the degree to which I truly trust my Creator. What I do know is my faith, my family, my marriage, my ministry, my writing, my joy—all daily depend on a hopeful posture from me. My work and yours is to build and rebuild our inner reserves of hope and then help others to do the same. Live in Hope—that is our mission.

Holy and Loving God,

I am fragile, flawed, perishable—
I am also light and love,
heaven sent and heaven bound,
a precious soul with infinite possibilities.
Help me discover the Divine shining through
my stardust.
Hope is there,
and love, true love.

Amen.

(Try praying this in your backyard one night this week while looking up to the stars.)

Write It Down

WRITING IS BOTH creative and cathartic. Transferring what is in your heart onto paper relieves stress, helps process trauma and loss and aids in healing, and supplies laughter and hope. You may surprise yourself how much you have inside to record and how much joy can be found using your creative muscles.

Twenty years ago, I started buying little lined-paper notebooks with pretty covers, some with leather and others with photos of paintings or lines of inspiring quotes. They have accumulated into a creative repository for my musings about everything from memories to ideas for new recipes, inspirations for my writings, quotes by artists or intellectuals, private prayers, and just crazy streams of consciousness.

Each of us is trying to make sense of the beautiful and the brutal of our own unique experiences and retain our hope. Something I find genuinely helpful is writing my thoughts down. Surprisingly, seeing them on paper provides clarity, awareness, and often a new way forward.

This week, use these questions to try your hand at writing.

1. What does hope look like for you? Create a list of hope-givers: a special person, a scripture, a song, or place. Refer back to your list when negative thoughts visit.

2. Be inspired by the wisdom of Emily Dickinson: "Not knowing when the Dawn will come, I open every Door." Write down a dream or hope that floats in secret between your head and heart. Next to it, jot down one thing you could do today to "open the door" to it becoming a reality.

3. Recall a joyous memory when you were overwhelmed by the feeling that life was good, full of beauty, and gave you reason to hope. How can you recapture that sense of awe and wonder?

31

New Ribbons

Sometimes just getting up and carrying on
is brave and magnificent.
—CHARLIE MACKESY

[Love] always protects, always trusts, always hopes,
always perseveres. Love never fails.
—1 CORINTHIANS 13:7–8 (NIV)

I am the oldest of six girls. Every morning of my childhood, my sisters and I would line up for my mom to braid our hair before walking to Pine Street School. In my mother's bedroom there was a beautiful mahogany armoire, and inside were rolls of grosgrain and satin ribbon in all the colors of the rainbow, along with several pairs of scissors. I can picture my mom now, measuring out the ribbon, cutting two equal pieces, and then tying them perfectly into bows on the ends of my braids. The ritual was like a blessing before sending me off to brave the world.

Inevitably, I would return home from school in disarray: I'd either be missing a ribbon or the ribbons that had made it home were dirty and fraying at the ends. The next morning, my mom would braid my hair once again and tie each with a brand-new ribbon. Happily, off I would go, fresh and excited for a new day.

How often do you feel like a ribbon fraying at the edges? This is a consequence to be expected in the roller-coaster reality of being human in an imperfect world. We can waste time and energy fighting change, or each morning we can begin anew, practice acceptance, and move on.

I believe God is always cutting a beautiful new ribbon, urging us forward, desiring us to be courageous in the face of an unknown future. Daily, we have the choice to cower or to be brave. The poet Rainer Maria Rilke tells us, "Perhaps all the dragons in our lives are princesses who are only waiting to see us act, just once, with beauty and courage." We get knocked down many times in this life, but we are created to rebound and embrace the next day. God built us to be resurrected.

"I dwell in possibility" is the first line of one of my favorite poems by Emily Dickinson. She writes about a vision of a house with infinite windows, rooms the size of cedar trees, and a roof that has no end. This metaphor demonstrates a vision for how she longed to approach her life, her faith, and her art. There are always possibilities to change course, discover something new, embrace a holier existence. As the years pass, if we are not careful, our lives can become small and claustrophobic. We see more roadblocks than possibilities. In the final line of the poem, Dickinson paints an image of her spreading wide her arms to gather paradise. Imagine if this was our daily posture: arms wide and heart open to divine possibility!

Everything is always more than it seems with God. Be patient with God's timing. Live your life confident that God has you, and one day you will find yourself in the province of joy again. I have Jeremiah's words memorized: "For I know the plans I have for you ... plans to give you hope and a future."* Let this be your rallying call too.

Blessed to wake for another day, you get new ribbons! Another chance. Be brave. God has something waiting for you today.

---

* Jeremiah 29:11, NIV

Divine One,

You are the love, the beauty,
and mercy in me.
The silent prayers, the living hope,
the awe and the wonder,
the creator and the dreamer in me,
the strength, the tenacity,
and surprising resilience in me.

You are the coordinates of heaven
mapped in my soul.
The softness, the quiet,
the reflective, the graceful.
All that is benevolent,
holy, and divine is You
abiding in me.

Remind me when I forget who I am—truly.
Human with a spark of divine.
Thank you for the gift of another day,
an incredible adventure lies before me.

Amen.

"*Lights in the Tunnels*"

THE LIVES AND writings of Thomas Merton, C. S. Lewis, Frederick Buechner, Mother Teresa, and Corrie ten Boom are some of the beacons of light in my own faith journey. I find it inspiring to hear their testimonies of faith: how they found their ways to God, what convinced them of a spiritual reality within and around them, and how faith led them through the "dark tunnels." Reading the experiences of other soulfull seekers, especially in their difficult seasons, wraps us in assurance. It is comforting to see how God was present in their lives, in the darkness as well as the light.

Following are five stirring stories of faith that give me hope. This week, journey to your local library or bookstore, or even look up a quote from one of these stories and see how it might inspire your soul.

Come Be My Light by Mother Teresa

The Seven Storey Mountain by Thomas Merton

Surprised by Joy by C. S. Lewis

The Hiding Place by Corrie ten Boom

Now and Then by Frederick Buechner

32

What I Know to Be True

Home is the center of my being where I can hear the voice
that says: "You are my Beloved, on you my favor rests"—the same
voice that . . . speaks to all the children of God and sets them free
to live in the midst of a dark world while remaining in the light.
—HENRI NOUWEN

If we love one another, God dwells deeply within us, and his love
becomes complete in us—perfect love!
—1 JOHN 4:12 (MSG)

Most people know Vincent van Gogh as the genius behind the paintings "Starry Night," "Bedroom in Arles," and "Sunflowers." But did you know that he was also the author of 820 letters that are today thought to be literary masterpieces of prose? They provide an oculus into the internal life of this artist, but even more, a testament to his faith. In a letter to his brother Theo dated September 3, 1882, van Gogh wrote, "It was only while painting it that I noticed how much light there was still in the dusk." Like every human, van Gogh searched for anchors of truth to ground him. He sought an eternal reality. He longed for evidence of the magnanimity and creativity of God.

It is challenging in our current age to decipher what is true and what can be trusted. Today we are bombarded with information, opinions, and perspectives. The most significant question, however, and one we should all ask ourselves, is "What does my soul know to be true?"

I believe we need anchors of belief to ground us and guide our lives when the earthly world seems so fragile, overwhelmingly secular, and lacking in hope. My spiritual anchors reveal who I believe God to be, who I am, what my holy purpose is, and what God promises me. Read through mine and see which ones resonate, and then create your own authentic list.

Spiritual Anchors

1. God is transcendent and immanent, and the guardian of my soul. God loved me first and will love me forever. All will eventually come together for good.

2. Jesus came to reveal God and show how to live a life of love.

3. The purpose of my life is to be a living expression of love in the world.

4. The surest way to a life of meaning is to make a difference in the life of another.

5. I am built to do brave things.

6. Prayer connects me to the One who gave me life (the Creator, God, Jesus, the Holy Spirit . . .) and I know that the One is listening and cares.

7. If you offer love for your gain or attach it with conditions—then it is not true love.

8. Refusal to forgive and show mercy makes me sick from the inside out. And may even shorten my life.

9. There isn't time to waste stressing about things that probably won't matter in two weeks' time. Daily, I must practice perspective.

10. God gave me others to help make my way. I will depend on friends, family, and community to sustain me, and I will reciprocate.

11. God desires me to feel joy often. Laughter is a gift.

12. There is nothing more marvelous and worth working toward than peace.

13. Life is a marathon. With God's help, I will never give up hope.

14. Hints of heaven are possible now, pointing to my eternal future.

Beloved,

Thank you for opening Your arms and whispering,
Come home.
To hope unyielding and love everlasting.
No matter how broken or bleak,
how deep and dark the hole,
heavy the cross,
long the winter,
Resurrection is Your signature.
The joy will return in the morning.
My soul will prevail;
You made her invincible.
I am Your beloved.

Amen.

Lectio Divina

THE BIBLE, NATURE, and human relationships have been my top three resources for knowing God and discerning God's desires for my life. The Bible offers a treasure of wisdom. If I were asked for a bibliography of my spiritual anchors, I would happily cite the Psalms, the book of Job, Paul's letters, and the Beatitudes. They are responsible for painting the portrait of God on my heart, and giving me a map for how to live a meaningful life. Reading the Bible can seem like a daunting proposition. Where do we begin?

We have St. Benedict of Nursa in the sixth century to thank for introducing his monastic community to the spiritual practice of Lectio Divina (translated from Latin: "Divine Reading"). It is a four-step process to explore the Bible for anchors of spiritual wisdom for present life. For this exercise, I have chosen Matthew 5:1–8, known as the Beatitudes or Jesus' Blessings, because it reveals how invested God is in the fine details of our daily lives.

This week, try beginning your own Lectio Divina:

Step One: Open to Matthew 5:1–8. I recommend Eugene Peterson's translation, *The Message*.

Step Two: Read the passage two or three times so the words have a chance to sink into your marrow.

Step Three: Sit quietly for three to five minutes and let the words float between your mind and heart. Silence other thoughts, worries.

Step Four: Begin an internal conversation between yourself and God about the passage. What comes bubbling up in your thoughts? Can meaning be gleaned here for your current personal life? Spend some time sitting contemplatively with the words. What do they tell you about God? How may these words inform your next steps?

Close with a sincere prayer of thankfulness.

33

Don't Be a Tourist in Your Own Life

I went to the woods because I wished to live deliberately,
to front only the essential facts of life, and see if I could learn
what it had to teach, and not, when I came to die,
discover that I had not lived.
—HENRY DAVID THOREAU

[May you] be filled with all the fullness of God.
—EPHESIANS 3:19 (NRSV)

Did you know that a family can actually "do" Yellowstone National Park in twenty-four hours? I have the photos to prove it: Old Faithful and the other major geysers, the waterfall and canyons, herds of bison and elk, bear tracks, moose crossings, eagle sightings, and peanut butter and jelly sandwiches with Pringles. We even played a Western mix tap with the family favorite "Oh, My Darling Clementine" in the car!

If it was printed in the guidebook, we did it. It was like we were on *The Amazing Race*, determined to see and do everything humanly possible in the shortest amount of time. Armed with cameras, bear spray, and gorp, we were the Great American Tourists!

But now when I think about it, the trip was a blur.

I don't want my life to be a blur.

Do you ever feel like you're a tourist in your own life? You are hitting the main attractions, crossing the T's, dotting the I's, and you even have the iPhone pictures to prove it. And yet you are moving so fast, trying to do everything at once, that you never really reside in your own life.

We live in a time when we are lauded for the greatest number of things that we can accomplish in one twenty-four-hour period. It's called the art of multitasking. Yet it comes at a high price. How many times have we found ourselves checking our phone, talking on the phone, calling out spelling words, and stirring the spaghetti sauce for dinner, all at once? If we are not careful, we will certainly miss something sacred. Multitaskers are never truly present in the moment. Life passes them by in a blur. Our culture has forgotten the art of relishing the moment.

My yoga instructor teaches *conscious practice* both on the mat and in daily living. Conscious practice is opening the five senses externally and your reflective soul internally to explore every aspect of life. I watched a marvelous documentary of a Zen master imparting deep life wisdom in his instruction on how to eat an orange. It took ages for him to finish the orange, but boy, did he enjoy it. First, he admired the fruit before him; then he put it up to his nose and reveled in its scent; and finally, ever so slowly, he peeled the orange, savoring each section. He left no doubt that every single cell of his body "experienced" that orange.

The Zen master knows life is not a twenty-four-hour trip to Yellowstone. It's meant to be explored and thoroughly savored in every cell of our being. I believe mindfulness, though it can feel elusive, is the secret to a balanced life. Washing the dishes, having a conversation with your nine-year-old, taking a shower, and walking the dog can become opportunities to experience the ordinary of our lives as a bit more sacred.

There are countless physical and emotional benefits in slowing down and being present in the moment. Mindfulness reduces hypertension, elevates cognitive abilities (memory), strengthens immune systems, and improves overall mental health. Not only does mindfulness provide a biological lift to our lives, but just as important, mindfulness transforms us into the calmer, gentler version of ourselves that we gift to our family, friends, and the world.

You are fooling yourself if you think life is just work promotions, carpool lines, to-do lists, and a perfectly chronicled photo library in your iCloud. We only get one ticket on this fast-moving train called Life. Slow down. Plan ahead and do not overbook yourself. There can be no guilt for prioritizing your soul and politely saying no. Schedule "unscheduled time" in your day to rest and renew. We owe it to ourselves, to the people we love, and to the world to be present, fully alive, and soul-attentive in every moment. There's nothing cool about being a tourist when you can be a resident in your own life!

Holy and Loving God,

The stay seems too short here;
help me focus on what matters.
Fill my earthly passport with adventure,
laughter,
goodness,
and
acts of courage.
You see, I'm practicing for heaven.

Amen.

Granola

The ritual of tying on my apron, opening my cookbook, taking out my ingredients, reaching for my wooden spoon, and following the steps of a recipe is a meditative practice for me. These "chapel experiences" in the kitchen slow me down, focus my attention, and bring me the reward of increased peace and joy. Meaningful life happens for me in the kitchen, whipping up something healthy for my family.

Something you will always find in my fridge is a mason jar full of my homemade granola. My husband, David, relishes it every morning for breakfast with almond milk and frozen blueberries. I snack on granola when I'm writing. The kids love a fancy parfait with layers of yogurt, honey, fresh berries, granola, and a sprig of fresh mint! Sometimes I even add pieces of dark chocolate for the adults and M&Ms for the kids to take for a day of fishing on the river or a jaunt in the woods.

Ingredients

½ cup raw honey, room temperature
½ cup coconut oil, melted
1 tbsp pure vanilla extract
6 cups raw oats
1 cup unsweetened shredded
    coconut (optional)
2 cups raw almonds, sliced

2 cups walnuts, chopped
2 cups raw cashews, chopped
1 cup raw sunflower seeds
1 cup pistachios, shelled
1 cup raw pumpkin seeds
2 tsp kosher salt
1 tbsp cinnamon

Directions

Preheat oven to 350°F. In one bowl, whisk together the wet ingredients. In another bowl, combine the dry ingredients and mix well. Fold the wet ingredients into the dry ingredients, and stir until everything is well coated. Spread the mixture onto a baking sheet, aiming for around ½-inch to 1-inch layer. Bake for 25 minutes, stirring regularly. I pull mine out on the earlier side because I prefer the granola not too toasty, but it's up to your own personal taste. Allow to cool for 20 minutes. Feel free to dress up your granola with dried Montmorency cherries, raisins, apricots, dates, or, if you are like me, dark chocolate chips!

34

The Little Way

Miss no single opportunity of making some small sacrifice,
here by a smiling look, there by a kindly word; always doing
the smallest right and doing it all for love.
—ST. THÉRÈSE OF LISIEUX

That you may live a life worthy of the Lord and please him
in every way: bearing fruit in every good work,
growing in the knowledge of God.
—COLOSSIANS 1:10 (NIV)

One of my favorite classes in divinity school focused on the lives of
the saints. We read about Francis of Assisi, Joan of Arc, Augustine,
Julian of Norwich, Catherine of Siena, and Mother Teresa. I especially
loved Marie-Francoise-Thérèse Martin. Today she is best known as St.
Thérèse of Lisieux, the "Little Flower."

At the age of nine, Thérèse decided to become a French nun. On a pilgrimage to Rome with her father, she had the pluck to ask Pope Leo XIII
for a special favor: to enter the Carmelite Order early. Her determination
paid off, and she took her vows of poverty, chastity, and obedience at the
age of fifteen. She had large dreams of doing something heroic, courageous, and adventurous for God, but she soon realized her life was des-
tined for the simple cloisters of a French convent in Normandy.

Little Flower did not wear the gleaming armor of Joan of Arc charging
into battle, nor did she travel as a missionary to exotic lands like St. Francis or live in the slums of India like Mother Teresa. But she was no less a

heroine of the faith. St. Thérèse followed her own sacred path, which she deemed the Little Way to God. Her beautiful spirituality consisted of doing small things with great love.

In the routine and ordinary of everyday life, Little Flower enthusiastically manifested God's love. Whether she was ringing the chapel bells, cleaning the altar, or washing clothes in the laundry room, she could make a difference. It was all about her attitude and willingness to increase goodness in her square inch of space. St. Thérèse proved that through the smallest gestures of kindness, the path of the saintly was open to her, and to ordinary folk like you and me.

A saint is one who allows the light to shine through them, dispelling a little of the world's darkness. Faced with adversity, they persevere and live in relentless hope. Dr. Cornel West said it best: "A saint ain't nothing but a flawed human being who looks at the world through the lens of the heart." We cannot live only for ourselves. The smallest gestures done with great love have the power to transform a moment, a very life.

Never underestimate the Little Way to God. Every day we have the opportunity to be generous, to love better and more often, and to bless the world as we have been blessed. This week, offer a smile instead of a frown. Be an encourager. Just listen. Healing is to be heard. Don't react to rudeness. Give the benefit of the doubt. Be generous with compliments. Make your last communication a word of hope.

Dear God,

I want my life to count for something more,
to be consequential in time, in space, and to someone,
hopefully a multitude.

So much effort has been given to acquisition
of place, knowledge, and treasure.
It's all part of the discovery.
Now I long for that which cannot be measured,
only shines.
Meaning comes in the giving away—
of the best of myself.

Let all the kindness in me be passed on,
every drop of mercy made into an oil for blessing,
my reserves of hope transferred to another,
my love blissfully spent, so
there is nothing left of me
but an incandescent soul.

I accomplished the mission.
Then I will be free, oh, so free,
to walk away from this world,
and begin another adventure of love.

Amen.

Small Acts of Kindness with Great Love

IN JUDAISM, THERE is a story I love about the gathering of the light called *Tikkun Olam*. As the story has been told, in the beginning there was one original source of Light, which supported the entire Universe. But something happened to shatter the light into infinite shards scattered across creation. Glimmers of this divine light are said to be found in every living thing, from majestic Sequoia trees to barking dogs, to soaring birds, to the beating human heart.

We are all called to search for the light, celebrate its presence, and then do whatever we can to increase it. The belief is that the simplest gestures of kindness can change outcomes. Each of us is assigned a tiny part of the world to make better.

Don't worry about numbers. Start with the person nearest you. This week, make it your daily mission to do one act of kindness that changes the day for another person.

35

One Flat Tire

In difficult times carry something beautiful in your heart.
—BLAISE PASCAL

For God gave us a spirit not of fear
but of power and love and self-control.
—2 TIMOTHY 1:7 (ESV)

After a mad morning rush of breakfast making, lunchbox packing, then scrambling to drop off five kids at three different schools, I was giddy to pull into the parking area of Radnor Lake. This day was to be my youngest, Finn's, introduction to a favorite sanctuary of mine. I tightened the straps and buckled him into the jogging stroller, attached a singing toy, and started up the hill. Not halfway up the ascent, I was dripping with sweat and huffing and puffing, surprised by the challenge of it. At the top of the hill, I stopped to catch my breath and survey the situation.

My jogging stroller is state-of-the-art and designed beautifully, especially for a runner. And I thought I was in pretty good shape, so what was holding me back? An older gentleman passed by me at a happy tortoise's pace and proffered, "I see your back tire is flat."

Quickly, I became as deflated as the left wheel of the jogging stroller. About to turn around and head back to the car, I had a revelation. The weather was perfect. The baby was happy. I had thirty minutes to myself. There were two other tires full of air. I pushed forward.

How often do you wake up to discover one of your metaphorical tires is flat?

No day on our planet is perfect. We must learn to roll with the unpredictability and fragility at every turn. According to Darwin, we succeed in life not by our intellect, or even our strength, but by our ability to adapt to the environment in which we find ourselves.

My friend has been battling cancer for as long as I have known her. You would never guess she has this very serious "flat tire." She knows that her limited time here on Earth is a quality-over-quantity journey. Her glow is contagious. I easily forget her "flat tire" because her soul is too busy shining like a beacon whenever we are together.

William Faulkner instructs, "Try to be better than yourself." He is calling us to rise above our flaws, our vulnerabilities, and our secret fears with courage. Thankfully, we don't have to do it alone. Grace is always available to us. The same God who created us, and knows the count of every hair on our heads, is invested in the fine details of our lives. Every step of the way, God is steering us to a fullness of life to exceed our wildest imaginations. We cannot allow a "flat tire" to stop us. Remember, God is the ultimate guardian of our path.

Those three miles around Radnor Lake pushing a loaded baby stroller with a wonky flat tire were a challenge. Not only was my pace slow, but my arms and legs screamed their discomfort. But I wouldn't have missed a moment. Nothing in life is ever going to be perfect. There will be days when we want to pull the covers over our heads and take a pass. But stop, survey the situation, and count your blessings. I guarantee you have enough in you to rise to the occasion.

Beloved,

Some days I feel lost and alone
in this dark winter world.
There is a shadow in this strange land.
It can eclipse my light,
throw me off hope's course,
thieve my joy.

It is easy to live from fear to fear.
Shrinking right before Your eyes.
What a waste of a precious life.

May Your angels rush in,
drawing back the curtain to reveal
You, effortlessly holding up the cosmos,
and my tender heart.
You come for me every time
and walk me back into the light.
Love, it is.

Amen.

Pesto

Let's face it! On those "one flat tire" kind of days, we need grace.
Let dinner be quick, easy, and a delicious reward for making it
through a challenging day or season. This is probably the most

requested recipe in my repertoire. It makes a double batch, so I can freeze half for a day when I am in a pinch for time but want to make sure my family has a healthy, delicious dinner.

Pesto pasta packs a mighty green health punch but also feels rich and rewarding! Homemade pesto is as good as the quality of your ingredients. This is where you splurge on an exceptional olive oil, authentic Italian Parmigiano-Reggiano, and just-picked basil! Finish with ribbons of grated Parmesan, a chiffonade of fresh basil, and fresh-ground pepper. Making a big bowl of pasta is the easiest way to host many around your table. Prepare for smiles!

Ingredients

5 cups basil
4 cups fresh spinach
2 cups Parmigiano-Reggiano, grated
1½ cups walnuts

½ cup olive oil, plus possibly another swirl at the end
juice of 1 lime
kosher salt and fresh-ground pepper

Directions

Combine all ingredients in a blender, but be careful not to add salt until tasting at the end, as the Parmesan lends its own salt. I use the lime for flavor but also to enhance the green color. My family loves this served over penne or spaghetti noodles, but any pasta works great. The pesto sauce can also be used to elevate chicken off the grill or to top a favorite appetizer of prosciutto wrapped around slices of cantaloupe.

36

Green Is My Color

Practice Resurrection.
—WENDELL BERRY

Forget the former things; do not dwell on the past. See, I am doing a
new thing! Now it springs up; do you not perceive it? I am making
a way in the wilderness and streams in the wasteland.
—ISAIAH 43:18–19 (NIV)

My sister bought an old, historic house in disrepair that she is now
renovating for her family. Most exciting was the discovery of a
forgotten secret garden enclosed inside a two-hundred-year-old stone
wall on the property. It was overgrown, a tangled mess of branches and
intimations of what once was. I asked, "How could the previous owners
have let this special place go?"

My imagination was captured by all the ways the old garden could be
resurrected. We could begin by pruning the warren of climbing roses and
the sprawling invasion of lilac. Next, maybe plant a few rows of fragrant
lavender and pungent rosemary, then turn the worn soil, sow grass seed,
and fertilize like crazy. The forgotten stalky hydrangeas could come back.
Finally, clean away the choking bramble to uncover the hidden bed of
lovely herbs. I saw so many possibilities for new life. Immediately, this
verse came to mind:

> *You will be like a well-watered garden, like a spring*
> *whose waters never fail.**

I believe this is how God looks upon us. Nothing sacred ever ends, it only waits to be transformed. Resurrection is our thankful reality.

Hildegard of Bingen,[†] a saint from the twelfth century, viewed the soul as a hidden garden needing to be faithfully tended. She wrote passionately of a "greening" of the spiritual acreage within us, essential to how we participate in the world outside of us. I am encouraged by Hildegard's imagery of a garden within. Regardless of what is happening outside of me, there is an expanse within where I can find beauty, peace, and infinite possibilities. It is the sanctuary of my soul.

The condition of my interior garden depends a lot on my discipline. I need quiet in my daily life, walks in nature, art inspiration (music, visual art, poetry), and the experiences of other spiritual seekers. I must pray and keep praying. Exercise and healthy nutrition are required. I must form a community of mutual love and support. I must commit time for my neighbor, give way to laughter and adventure. Above all, I need love, given and received. The "greening" of me depends on my willingness to let old perspectives die and welcome new ones, burying grudges and holding fast to hope. The miracle of a well-watered internal garden is that it will inevitably and happily spill out like a lush vine over the stone wall and through the gate, transforming our external reality: relationships, careers, and our vision of the world.

---

*   Isaiah 58:11, NIV
†   Saint Hildegard of Bingen was a Renaissance polymath living at the beginning of the twelfth century: abbess, writer, composer, philosopher, theologian, scientist, healer, saint. She is revered as the founder of scientific natural history in Germany.

Is your life like my sister's forgotten garden? Take heart; nothing is beyond God's reach to give new life. Resurrection is beautifully coded in the programming of every living thing, from a minuscule blade of grass to the extraordinary human soul. God's blueprint for revival also extends to relationships, perspectives, faith, and dreams.

Always God is waiting to work a new thing in your life and mine. Nothing is final; however your inner garden and exterior life appear at this moment in time, know that God is sitting at the garden gate ready to work a miracle on your plot of potential green. Roll up your sleeves and open your heart.

Beloved,

It's a day like any other day,
except what if it's not?
What if I woke up today
and saw the world as enchanted?
What if I unfurled my tight grip and welcomed—
actually, begged—
You to do something new in my life?

Amen.

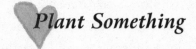

Plant Something

Show me your garden and I shall tell you what you are.
—ALFRED AUSTIN

JOY IS FOUND in watching something you planted grow and flourish, especially when it gifts you with blossoms, fruit, perfume-scented air, or sublime beauty outside your kitchen window. This week, let's plant something. It could be a ginkgo tree, a hydrangea bush, daffodil bulbs for next spring, tomato vines, culinary and medicinal herbs, or a cutting garden of zinnias. Let yourself be surprised by the joy that comes with watching something new grow.

I am a fan of the French "potager" or kitchen garden. This is a beginner's foray into gardening but with a huge payoff. In a tin planter, I arrange an herb medley of mint, oregano, verbena, thyme, rosemary, sage, chamomile, and basil. I make calming teas of verbena leaves and chamomile flowers, prepare the most delicious tomato mozzarella salads with my fragrant basil, and use sage as my secret ingredient in my delicious grilled chicken skewers. When I feel like I am walking on "eggshells" in the world, clipping rosemary, basil, and chamomile right outside my kitchen door returns me to a place of peace and possibility.

37

Follow Your Bliss

Your life is already artful, waiting, just waiting, for you to make it
art.
—TONI MORRISON

This is the day that the Lord has made; let us rejoice and be glad in it.
—PSALM 118:24 (ESV)

Albert Einstein was a world-renowned physicist and Nobel Prize winner, whose fame was based on his theory of relativity. But did you know that in private he was a self-taught violinist whose bliss was playing Mozart, Bach, and Beethoven? Einstein, with his beloved violin, "Lina," hosted homespun concerts every Wednesday night with his friends. He said playing music was the inspiration for every significant accomplishment in his life and his greatest source of joy. Music was where he could dream and experience bliss.

Creativity is a gift, a holy opportunity. We are made in God's image, which means embedded within us is the DNA to create. Although we don't have the talent or power to produce a magnificent universe, or a one-in-a-million unique fingerprint, we are petite creators in our own rights with a unique destiny. The language of the artist is in us. Creating beauty in any form is near sacramental. How marvelous to tap into our divinity through our imaginations.

Are you afraid of following your bliss? Creative expression is not just reserved for the likes of a Chagall, a Vivaldi, or a da Vinci. One stumbling block to creative endeavors is a culture that celebrates mastery and perfection, dollar signs and accolades, over passion and simple joy. Somewhere along the way, we have lost the balance of work and play. We experience guilt when we step away from the grind of life's responsibilities to pursue the dream-seeking parts of our beings. And yet it's the activation of our creative sweet spot that makes life magical.

Following our bliss invites delight, wonder, and a break from the seriousness and structure of our daily lives. We have to step away from our routines and do something that invites joy into our lives. I have a friend whose day job is working in a bookstore, but if you followed her on Instagram, you would know her bliss is baking elaborate and beautiful cakes. Another special friend slips away after feeding her children dinner and takes a classical ballet class every Tuesday night. She's over forty, but when she's pirouetting, she becomes ageless.

In an interview, Steven Pressfield, author of *The War of Art*, makes a distinction between the life we live and the untapped life within us. That life is right there gestating, waiting for us to open the door. The soul is a veritable dream factory. Try dancing, cooking, painting, speaking French, gardening, ballroom dancing, doing yoga, playing the piano, knitting, throwing pottery, kneading bread, writing—all a soul at play! When we contribute these sparks of creativity to the world, there is a lovely domino effect of joy on the community of souls.

Regularly, do something that puts you into the flow, where your mind is turned off and you are just in the moment doing something that gives you joy. Howard Thurman's prophetic words serve as our rallying call: "Ask yourself what makes you come alive, and go do that, because what the world needs is people who have come alive!"

Follow your bliss.

Creator of me,

There is no time
to squander.
My soul has its
destiny to fulfill.
Create.
Hope.
Love.
Repeat.

Amen.

Live to One Hundred Salad

Cooking is where I channel my inner Picasso! The kitchen is my atelier, or artist's studio. I read cookbooks as if they are novels. Although I do not cook from recipes, they inspire my culinary imagination. Many years ago, a friend nicknamed me the Salad Queen for my creative, colorful, and delicious salads. No two of my salads are alike. I always include avocado as my butter and Parmesan or another cheese for my salt! Creating a salad for me is truly an artistic endeavor. I have penned this my "Live to One Hundred Salad" because every ingredient contributes to a healthy mind, body, and spirit.

Salad Ingredients

a mélange of salad greens
    (arugula, romaine, spinach,
    purple endive)
1 cup Italian parsley, chopped
½ cup fresh mint, chopped
½ cup fresh basil, chopped
1 cup roasted hazelnuts
½ cup raw pumpkin seeds
1 cup dried Montmorency cherries
1 apple or pear, sliced thin
1 avocado, sliced
2 sweet potatoes, washed and
    chopped into cubes
kosher salt and black pepper
½ cup Parmigiano-Reggiano,
    grated for sweet potatoes

olive oil
1 cup farro, cooked
1 cup green lentils, cooked
2 boiled organic eggs
½ cup Mediterranean olives
1 cup cilantro, chopped
juice of 1 lime
Parmigiano-Reggiano ribbons
    (shaved using a vegetable
    peeler)
½ loaf of rosemary-olive, raisin/
    cranberry walnut, or sourdough
    bread, cubed for croutons

Dressing Ingredients

⅓ cup raw organic apple cider
    vinegar
½ cup high-quality olive oil
3 tbsp maple syrup or honey

1 tsp herbes de Provence
Juice of ½ lemon
salt and pepper

Directions

Preheat oven to 450°F. In a mason jar, mix all dressing ingredients and shake. Set aside. Place cubed sweet potatoes on a parchment-covered baking sheet, drizzle with olive oil, grated Parmigiano-Reggiano, kosher salt, and ground pepper, and bake for 15 minutes. Let them cool and then generously dress with cilantro, lime juice, and black pepper. Cut up bread of choice into bite-size chunks. Coat with olive oil, herbes de

Provence, kosher salt, and ground pepper. Throw into the oven on broil for 3-5 minutes. Allow to cool.

Be creative in how you arrange your beautiful salad. Start with your colorful salad greens; add your sweet potatoes, avocado, olives, sliced pears, farro, lentils, hazelnuts, pumpkin seeds, and boiled egg. Decorate the top with all your fresh herbs, Parmigiano-Reggiano ribbons, and homemade croutons. Toss with your healthy apple cider dressing, and serve.

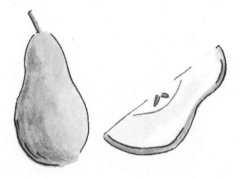

38

Kintsugi

We are full of paradise without knowing it.
—THOMAS MERTON

I can do all things through Christ who strengthens me.
—PHILIPPIANS 4:13 (NKJV)

Kintsugi is the ancient Japanese art of repairing broken porcelain with gold lacquer. It originated in the late fifteenth century when the Japanese shoguns sent their damaged pottery back to China to be restored. They ordered it not to be mended with the traditional metal staples but instead with real gold. It has since become a beautiful art form. What a revelation. An object becomes more beautiful from having been broken and mended.

We humans were created just like these perfect porcelain vessels, true Artist's masterpieces. Sadly, it only takes a few slips here on Earth before life tests the strength of our being. Slowly, often imperceptibly, little fissures appear on the surface of our spirit. Broken dreams, broken bodies, broken relationships, broken faiths, a whole broken world—try to damage us beyond repair.

The art of faith is committing to mend our brokenness so that we can move forward and fulfill our holy purposes here on Earth. Unfortunately, some of us try to mend the cracks with some very weak staples of our own. We rely on crutches like alcohol, or descend into bitterness and despair. We forget that it takes time, perseverance, aid from those who love us, and trust in the Beloved for our minds, bodies, and souls to be healed.

Have you ever met a person who has suffered the worst consequences in life, and yet somehow they mysteriously glow? They are more beautiful because of their brokenness and stronger for having endured the heartbreak? With courage and hope, these people walk the path from suffering to healing, determined to see their way out of the wilderness into a new province of joy. The journey transforms them into authentic spiritual luminaries, whose light helps others navigate through their own suffering. They show us that resilience is beautiful.

There is no avoiding cracks in the porcelain of our humanity. Crushing days will shatter us. Heartbreaks will happen. We will feel the fragility of our bodies. And wonder where God is. Breaking and mending is part of every human story. We fall and rise, hurt and heal, die and resurrect, so that we can continue to participate, grow, take our fill of joy, and accomplish our special destiny.

Open yourself to God's holy kintsugi.

Divine One,

You are not afraid of my flaws and imperfections
but instead embrace them.
Tenderly, You mend my broken places
with Your gold,
making me stronger, braver, wiser,
and more beautiful than before.
In the breaks and shattering,
I realize, with Your help,

how resilient I can be.
Next time my porcelain suffers a crack,
help me to not be so afraid,
Your Love is on the way.
That is Your promise.

Amen.

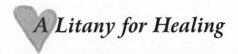 A Litany for Healing

WE EACH HAVE some contour in our lives in need of healing. Spiritual kintsugi begins the moment we invite God into our pain and brokenness. Love is the cure. Be open and patient for all the ways God is working to make you whole again, stronger than before. Try following this litany as a way to commend your body, mind, and spirit to God so healing can begin. Pray the regular text silently; say the **bolded** text aloud.

Place your hand on your heart, read the litany, and take your fill of the hope necessary to rise for today.

Allow me to see a glimmer of hope breaking through
my darkness.
Show me the way.

Touch me in my deepest need, in spirit and body.
Reassure me that You are a God of hope and
resurrections, small and grand.
Make healing my present reality.

Help me see that I am more than my fragile body or my
spirit challenged by doubt or my fears for what
is to come.
Have mercy on me.

Teach me to let go of my need for control so there is space
for Your mystery and grace to transform circumstances
and outcomes.
Reveal Your holy and grounding presence.

Help me to quiet the noise of the outside world and the
secret fears that overwhelm from the inside so Your
peace can enter in and renew me.
Be Still, I will. And Know that You are my God.

Renew my courage, touch the wick of my inner spirit so
that my light can be strong again, bolster my hope
and renew my trust in Your plan for my life.
In You, I live, move, and find my being.

Help me accept by faith that You dwell deep within my
soul, and nothing—not my fears, not my doubts,
not my flaws, not my brokenness—can separate me
from You.
Thank you for a Love deeper than any I know.

39
How Much for a Hug?

It is said that each time we embrace someone warmly,
we gain an extra day of life.
—PAULO COELHO

For I am convinced that neither death nor life, neither angels
nor demons, neither the present nor the future, nor any powers,
neither height nor depth, nor anything else in all creation,
will be able to separate us from the love of God.
—ROMANS 8:38–39 (NIV)

Walking along the Santa Monica Pier in Los Angeles on a warm Saturday afternoon, I came upon a serendipity: Mikey's Deli. This was not your ordinary deli, serving corned-beef hash or hot dogs loaded with mustard and sauerkraut. Mikey's Deli served hugs. For the price of two sincere compliments, you got to enjoy a hug. On the menu at the Hug Deli, one could order a Warm and Fuzzy Hug, a Bear Hug, a Group Hug, even a Beverly Hills Air Kiss Hug. Mikey created the deli as an "interactive art installation" to promote the benefits of hugging. Following the instructions on the green sign, I went behind the counter, put on the waiting apron, and then asked my husband David for his order. We giggled like kids. He ordered a Bear Hug with a kiss on the side!

This roller-coaster ride of life can be daunting, especially when faced alone. Our culture is especially plagued by anxiety and loneliness. We need all the hugs and serendipitous moments of affection we can get.

After the September 11 terrorist attack in New York City, my church set up a program through which members could adopt families who had suffered from the tragedy. My husband and I were paired with a single mother and her two sons. The two precious little brothers had been on the playground that day near the Twin Towers and watched as men and women jumped to their deaths. It would forever change their lives. I remember the first time they came to our apartment. There was an awkward silence. The family remained politely quiet during the spaghetti supper and barely smiled after the dessert of chocolate cake and ice cream.

Fear was the gigantic white elephant in our tiny, shoebox apartment. And then something wonderful happened. We introduced the boys to our Bijon puppy, Louis! He was a master of nuzzles and wet-nose kisses. My best friend had gifted Louis a Superman cape for Christmas, which he hilariously kept getting tangled up in. The room was filled with giggles. A tiny miracle. The boys felt a flicker of joy again. Hope returned. Louis had saved the day!

I have spent a great deal of my studies at seminary and within my present church ministry trying to understand what healing looks like on this side of heaven. I have learned the hard lesson that healing is not always a cure or an answer to the whys of suffering. Deep healing is made possible when we surrender to a higher power and open our hearts to one another. A hug or word of encouragement transforms people and outcomes for good. Jesus was a master at embracing the physical and spiritual suffering of humanity. Every time he reached out to touch someone, he offered a healing that transcended the temporal body. He spent his earthly life hugging and touching the blind, the leper, the sinner, and the saint.

The French word for hug is *embrasser*. *Je t'embrasse*. "I embrace you." This is a soul need, to have our entire being embraced by God, and by others near and far. God gave us each other to see our earthly way through. Let's not be stingy with expressions of love. Instead, let's open our arms and embrace one another. The poet William Blake said it beautifully: "We are put on earth [for] a little space, that we may learn to bear the beams of love." This whole magnificent planet of ours needs a great, big bear hug (or a wet-nose kiss from Louis!).

Holy One,

Your Spirit lives within me.
My life's work is to reveal it.
Today I love
not carefully, quietly,
or just enough,
but with a radical largeness,
that in a twinkling breath,
Heaven is brought to Earth.
For them,
and for me.

Amen.

Moelleux au Chocolat (Chocolate Cake)

Chocolate is just plain good for the body and the soul! For the chocolate connoisseur, there is nothing as delicious as the famous French dessert moelleux au chocolat, or in layman's terms, the flourless chocolate cake! What makes this dessert so delectable is the exciting moment the spoon breaks through the crust to a warm chocolate-mousse center! I must confess that I'm an amateur baker on my best day. If the old kitchen adage is true, that "cooking is an art, baking is a science," I'm in trouble even before the egg white and yolk part ways and the butter and sugar are creamed. Trust me, this recipe will give you confidence! Not only are there just four main ingredients (chocolate, egg whites, sugar, and cream of tartar), but cooking time is 12 minutes, and these cakes are gluten-free. *Heavenly* is the only word to describe this dessert. Enjoy with a friend!

Ingredients

10 oz high-quality dark chocolate, at least 65% cacao (I suggest one bag of Ghirardelli's dark chocolate chips)

6 extra-large organic egg whites (the fresher the eggs, the better)

½ tsp cream of tartar

½ tsp fine sea salt

6 tbsp fine cane sugar

coconut oil

powdered sugar, for dusting

6 oven-proof ramekins

Directions

Preheat oven to 350°F. There are three steps to this recipe: The first is the art of melting the chocolate. Chocolate does not like direct, high heat. Therefore, you must use a bain-marie (double-boiler) or, like me, improvise. Use a saucepan filled with a couple inches of boiling water, set a heat-proof bowl containing the chocolate chips over it, trying your best not to allow the bowl to touch the water. Slowly, stir the chocolate chips until they are melted. Remove the bowl from the heat and set aside.

Next, separate your egg whites. No yellow allowed! In either a standing mixer fitted with a whisk or using a hand-held mixer, combine the egg whites, cream of tartar, and salt. Beat the egg-white mixture until it is frothy, then slowly add the sugar on medium-high speed until you reach stiff peaks. (It should look like stiff whipped cream.)

With a spatula or large spoon, delicately fold dollop after dollop of the egg-white mixture into the melted chocolate. Do not rush this process or stir vigorously, or else your beautiful egg whites will turn to soup. Next, grease 6 ramekins with coconut oil and fill each halfway with your chocolate mixture. Place in your preheated oven. Bake the mini chocolate cakes until the tops crack, about 12 minutes. Transfer to a rack to cool for 5 minutes before serving. Dust the tops with powdered sugar, and voilà, you have a three-star moelleux au chocolat! Now all you have to do is close your eyes and imagine you are sitting in a Parisian café on the Left Bank with Edith Piaf playing in the background!

40

Faith Gazing

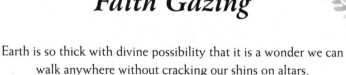

Earth is so thick with divine possibility that it is a wonder we can
walk anywhere without cracking our shins on altars.
—BARBARA BROWN TAYLOR

The heavens declare the glory of God; the skies proclaim
the work of his hands.
—PSALM 19:1 (NIV)

A Perseid meteor shower occurs every year. It happens when Earth
passes through the lovely celestial trail of the Swift-Tuttle comet.
Shooting stars occur when pieces of stardust (some the size of a grain of
sand) burn up as they enter the Earth's atmosphere, leaving a streak of
light across our night sky.

The year 2016 was a much-publicized one in astronomical circles due
to an unusually strong gravitational pull of the planet Jupiter toward
Earth. Scientists anticipated a double dose of star power. At the peak of
that particular year's star storm, NASA promised the sky would spill with
stars, predicting two hundred shooting stars a minute.

I gathered my family and headed for the beach on an August evening
to witness this cosmic event in all its hyped glory. Single file, we made our
way down the boardwalk in the pitch black and took our places under a
vast and majestic sky.

My three- and five-year-olds quickly lost patience and turned their
attention to hunting crabs and sea turtles in the dunes. Suddenly, my

husband pointed and called out, "Shooting star!" My eldest teen whispered next to me, "That was cool." Elise, my budding scientist, announced, "This is like the Fourth of July!" Craning my neck and scanning around back and forth, I searched the night canopy for my own celestial sign.

Nothing—a shutout for Mom! And the next night too. Again, nothing. Apparently, the night sky was to become my classroom on faith.

A professor at Vanderbilt University Divinity School described faith to me as *persevering from the last time you heard or experienced God until the next time.*

In secret, who among us wouldn't love some black-and-white proof? A supernatural sign, a surprise shooting star, an angelic visitation. We are modern-day doubting Thomases,* longing to touch the supernatural to believe. In this Amazon-one-click culture, we expect "glory" at the snap of a finger or a quick swipe across the screen. But just as the resplendent cosmos confounds astronomers, God remains an infinite mystery to the human mind and heart.

God's presence in my own life has proved to be more whispers and nudges. But you string a couple of these together and suddenly you have a beautiful constellation of hope. Faith, for me, is living one glimmer to the next. A soul-engaged faith is a lifelong search for God: No easy answers. Patience required. Grace promised.

The irony in astronomy and in life is that the darker the night, the greater the chance of seeing shooting stars and witnessing God. We all have dark nights, convinced there is not a single star in our sky. But wait . . . just wait. God is near and faith is constellating inside us. Dare to

---

* "Doubting Thomas," sometimes referred to as "Honest Thomas," was one of Jesus' disciples who struggled to believe in the resurrection without physical proof. Jesus appears to Thomas and invites him to touch his wounds. Jesus says to Thomas, "Blessed are those who have not seen and yet have come to believe" (John 20:29, NRSV).

trust that God is in control and has a wondrous, redeeming, and loving plan in place, even if we cannot see it now.

On the third and final night, we all returned to the beach, searching the heavens for a bit of stardust. I sat for hours stargazing. Just as I was about to give up for the night, a streak of light shot across the sky (I learned these types of shooting stars are called "Earth grazers," because they display an especially long, colorful streak). I was speechless. My husband looked in my direction with a smile. "Saved the best for last!"

To live soulfully is to believe that something larger than oneself, something marvelous, is at work in this world. It is our job to open our eyes to see it—to participate in it. Sometimes it's barely a whisper after months of gazing in the dark. But the wait is worth it, because God will surprise us with a message written in stardust across our night skies declaring: "I am here!"

God of the stars and of
my beating heart,

May my life reflect the Truth:
Hope is real.
Healing is possible.
Life is a privilege.
I exist for a purpose.
Grace is available.
Love prevails.
You have me.
I am moving toward the Eternal.

Amen.

One Hundred Blessings

ONE WAY WE can live from one glimmer to the next is by welcoming a gravitational shift in our perspective. Beautiful living happens when we try to locate God in every hour of our day. This is a worthy spiritual discipline. What a surprise and relief to find that there is not a single sky in our lives without a star!

In Judaism, the *berakhot,* or "prayer of blessings," is a special kind of gratitude practice. Jewish tradition calls an observant Jew to pray one hundred blessings a day! Every *berakah* begins, "Blessed are you, Lord our God, King of the Universe, who . . ." And then you make it personal. I might pray: ". . . blessed me with a husband who still grabs my hand as we drift off to sleep, blessed me with five sisters who make me laugh, blessed me with a mom who chooses to see the best in me, blessed me with a clear night to see the stars."

Another way to practice this is to write down three things you are grateful for before your first cup of coffee every morning. Not only does it start the day on the right foot, but it also ensures a smidgen more of humility and hope for whatever the day's circumstances bring. Gratitude invites grace into our lives.

Make it your daily practice: three to one hundred thank-yous or *berakhot* a day.

41

Jenga

We must feel that we are supported by that same process that
brought the Earth into being, that power that spun the galaxies
into space, that lit the sun and brought the moon into its orbit.
—THOMAS BERRY

Behold, I am with you and will keep you wherever you go . . . For I will
not leave you until I have done what I have promised you.
—GENESIS 28:15 (ESV)

Have you ever played the game Jenga? It begins with a tower constructed from fifty-four blocks. The object is to remove individual blocks without the tower collapsing. Every time a piece is removed by a player, the structure becomes more unsteady. Jenga is an apt metaphor for the human experience. We are these marvelous strongholds, but inevitably the realities of life shake our internal structure, and what we believe to be true and trustworthy.

Faced with scary pandemics, unjust wars, refugee crises, and natural disasters in the forms of fire, flood, and tornado, plus losing friends and family to cancer, I have found myself wondering, "Where are you, God?" or "Creator God, Your beautiful world is coming undone. Do something." and "Now, God!"

Recently, I visited a young mother losing her battle against breast cancer. I crawled into the bed with her three young children to help them say goodbye to her. When I left I felt a large Jenga block loosen in my heart and disturb my spiritual foundation. Then another block tumbled down after the death of my friend Daniel. He was forty-two, again with young children, stricken with complications from COVID-19. Eighteen years ago, Daniel saved the day for us when our son Charlie was diagnosed with cancer. He gave my husband a consulting job at his company, which allowed him the flexibility to be at home or the hospital during Charlie's treatments. Next, my shaky tower received a knockout blow with the devastating loss of my dear friend Tallu from terminal brain cancer.

These events happened so close together that I found myself asking: Is my determination to believe and hope simply a deceit? Yet something still, small, and not of this world—deep inside me—refused to give in to this despair. I remembered that God cannot be toppled—which means you and I cannot be toppled.

Herbert McCabe, a theologian I greatly admire, avows this fundamental truth of our mortal existence: We are loved by God. He said if we know in our depths that we are loved by God, then nothing—not our darkest night, not our greatest loss, not our most frightening doubt, not our pain, not our suffering, not even our deaths—can fully collapse our "towers."

In Jesus' moment of utter despair on the cross, God stepped in, and God will somehow step in for us too. Maybe it doesn't happen at the moment we think logical or imperative. We may never be given dramatic, tangible proof, but when you love something, you step in and save the tower from toppling.

My Jenga tower and yours are secure in God's love.

Dear God,

How do I make peace with the Unfair
(the cruel)?
Why must a heart be broken?
I conjure so many different outcomes—
Where mothers do not lose children
and children do not lose mothers.
Where no one is hungry and war is dropped from the
common lexicon.
Where everyone knows the exquisite experience of loving
and being loved.
Today, my daughter asked me how I could still believe—
Like me, she painfully absorbs
the world's hurts deep inside.
I told her the truth:
None of us is safe from the fate of Jesus,
Nor thankfully—from His destiny.
Dear God, please step in and save the day,
we both know there is much good to be saved.
I am holding You to Your promise
for Love to find a way.
Make good on Your word
For her, for me, for all.

A hopeful Amen.

One-Pot Wonder Soup

This is a recipe for the most comforting pot of soup! Imagine a warm, weighted blanket in a dark, cold winter season. It might be responsible for a missing Jenga piece restored. The truth is, the lentil soup is a delicious and soul-filling gift in all seasons. Bonus: This soup is even better the next day! I also use the leftover lentils as a base for a simple arugula and avocado salad with a squeeze of lime for lunch during the week.

When a close friend finalized her divorce, I showed up unannounced with my one-pot wonder and an enclosed note: *It is time to write a new chapter. Follow where Love leads you.* This week, consider who in your life might need a one-pot wonder delivered unannounced, and watch how the joy of giving might restore a Jenga block in your own life too.

Ingredients

1 onion, diced
2 leeks, chopped (washed and trimmed; use white and green parts)
2 cups celery, diced
1 cup carrots, diced
1 bay leaf
3 tbsp coconut oil
1 tbsp herbes de Provence
kosher salt
fresh-ground pepper
32 oz vegetable or chicken stock (bone broth is a bonus!)

4 cups water
1 box (17.6 oz) Le Puy green lentils (I like the French brand Sabarot)
1 tsp cinnamon
1½ tsp cumin
2 tsp turmeric
1 rind of Parmigiano-Reggiano
1 can (13.5 oz) organic coconut milk
1 bag fresh spinach, chopped
1 cup Italian parsley, chopped, plus more for garnish
juice of 1 lime

Directions

In a soup pot, begin sautéing your mirepoix of onion, leeks, celery, carrots, and bay leaf in the coconut oil. Season with herbes de Provence and kosher salt. Cook until the onions are translucent. Pour in your stock, water, lentils, cinnamon, cumin, turmeric, and Parmigiano rind. Stir to blend the flavors. Cover and allow to simmer for 45 minutes. Turn off heat and stir in the coconut milk. Fold in fresh spinach and parsley. Squeeze lime juice into pot. Salt and pepper to taste. Garnish with fresh herbs. Crisp a baguette in the oven and serve with dishes of olive oil.

A great addition: Choose an organic sausage. My family likes organic chicken-and-apple sausage. Slice into medallions and then sauté for 2 minutes. Add into the soup before serving.

42

What Truly Matters

For any spirit suddenly awakened to how deep its life
how short its stay.
—MARK NEPO

And above all these, put on love, which binds everything together
in perfect harmony.
—COLOSSIANS 3:14 (ESV)

At Larkspur Conservancy in Westmorland, Tennessee, I participated in the most beautiful natural burial of my friend Tallu Quinn. There was music, fields of wildflowers, and heart-shaped rocks placed with love around the opening in the earth. Tallu's body was wrapped in a shroud handmade by her dear friend Margo, and it was laid on a bed of flowers arranged to look like a sunset at her beloved Jekyll Island.

Tallu lost a fierce battle against brain cancer at the age of forty-one. She used every bit of the time she was given on this Earth to build a consequential life, sacred, with love as the driving purpose. She was a *New York Times* best selling author, mother, wife, artist, activist, and friend who made a huge impact on so many in her short time on Earth. Her life has become my cherished map for how I wish to live mine going forward.

Tallu was a master at pulling tiny pieces of heaven down to Earth. No matter how disappointing or heartbreaking the circumstance, my friend found her way back into the province of hope. To leave her presence was to take with you some of her glow, and a renewed confidence that love would have the last word and God could be trusted. She was practicing for heaven for as long as I knew her by the way she lived and loved. At Tallu's funeral, a gentleman I didn't know leaned over and said to me, "Many will live to be ninety like me and never come close to achieving as holy a life as Tallu did."

We are given an unknown measure of time under heaven's rim to figure out how to love and be loved, to forgive and show mercy, to grow and finally to die. If we are doing it right, we will discover, as my friend Tallu did, that love carries us through it all.

In her memoir, *What We Wish Were True*, Tallu leaves us with gentle marching orders: "We have to practice what we hope for. As if what we hope for might be possible." She was a master at this. She was one of those people who always elevated the conversation and made it sacred. Over the years, both of us felt God's presence together laughing barefoot in our kitchens, chopping herbs, filling bud vases with wildflowers, stirring big pots of soup, and pulling up as many chairs as possible around our dining tables. Tallu had a special talent for holding life's joys and sorrows together at once in her heart, never allowing either to completely overtake her. She could see a sliver of light in the darkest dark and find pleasure in the smallest joy.

Like Tallu, I am going to practice what I hope for. I want to meet each day with a pure heart. I desire to be known and remembered for my love. I will search for experiences of heaven now and as glimpses of my promised future. I want to laugh, pray, weep, grieve, forgive, grow, and create to my last breath. I will practice daily trusting God and gratefully acknowledging that all of it is a gift.

What do you hope for?

Holy One,

Instead of looking for life's answers,
I'm just going to look for You, my God,
in all and everything.
Love will be my only religion.
I'm going to wear out my welcome here on Earth.
I'll show up at heaven's door,
my humanity in tatters,
no stone left uncovered or bottle uncorked.
Let the angels speak about the way I loved,
bear-hugged every moment,
gave You my all and more.
At the bell tolling, I hope to hear You say,
"That was a life worth My breath."

Amen.

Reading Poetry as a Spiritual Practice

MY FRIEND TALLU introduced me to the reading and savoring of poetry as a spiritual discipline. For fifteen years, we gifted each other poems that had struck a soulchord within us—the poetry of Rainer Maria Rilke, John O'Donohue, Mary Oliver, Denise Levertov, and Wendell Berry, to name just a few. Wonderfully, the language of poetry has brought new depth and color to the liturgy of my personal spiritual life.

In so few words, a poem can reveal the mind and heart of God. The first time I read the luminous words of the Sufi poet Rumi I had such a revelation. His poem "The Guest House" is therapy in eighteen lines. Rumi's poetry inspired me to look for God outside my own traditions. The poet Mary Oliver taught me to encounter God in the ordinary of my life, especially in nature. Her "The Summer Day" is a rallying call to relish and honor the life we have been given. The poet Rainer Maria Rilke's words inspire me to lean into God when life feels more challenge than glory. Denise Levertov's poem "The Thread" assures me that whatever happens, I am eternally connected by a sacred thread to God.

I believe an expanding and creative spiritual life requires openness to all the curious ways God is speaking into creation. Poetry continues to be an exciting addition to my faith.

The following are some of my favorite poems. This week, I challenge you to look these up and try to commit to memorizing a line or two.

Mary Oliver: "The Summer Day," "Thirst"
Denise Levertov: "The Thread," "The Avowal"
William Stafford: "The Way It Is"
Emily Dickinson: "Some Keep the Sabbath Going to Church"
Rainer Maria Rilke: "Go to the Limits of Your Longing"

43

Your Cornerstone

You thought you were being made into a decent little cottage: but
[God] is building a palace.
—C. S. LEWIS

Look, I have laid a stone . . . a tested stone, a precious cornerstone, a
sure foundation; the one who believes will be unshakable.
—ISAIAH 28:16 (CSB)

On an auspicious morning in the year 1163, two men stood in the
rarefied French dust of what would one day become the site of the
great gothic Cathedral of Notre Dame. One was a bishop, the other,
the Pope of Christendom. Together they sprinkled holy water, read from
the Psalter, dedicated a block of smooth stone, and sang the beautiful
canticle "Veni Creator Spiritus." This was no ordinary rock hastily un-
earthed from a northern French quarry but the very "cornerstone" of
Paris's beloved Notre Dame Cathedral.

On any eighteenth-century map of France, all roads began and ended
at Notre Dame's steps. Not only is she an architectural wonder of stone
and jeweled glass, but this grand lady has survived revolutions, world
wars, reigns of terror, and lately tragic fires—proving that she was built
with a solid foundation.

The cornerstone is the first and most important stone laid in the construction of any building. All others are calculated from this central point.
It sets the tone for the work of art to come. In medieval cathedrals, the

cornerstone was placed at the heart of the cruciform design, the spot reserved for the holy altar.

In the very beginning of you and me, God laid an otherworldly cornerstone, our beautiful and indestructible soul, designed to rest in the "altar position" of our hearts. And we learn in Ecclesiastes that God set eternity there.*

Some dismiss that lovely original design and instead try to lay a cornerstone of wealth, popularity, beauty, or cleverness to anchor their lives. Such a false edifice has a flimsy foundation. Imperceptible to the human eye, invisible fissures soon begin to form. We do our best to hide our flawed vaults, weak arches, and crumbling marble. But eventually this compromised structure shudders under the weight of our misaligned priorities and weak cornerstone.

But remember, we were designed to prevail, to be like Notre Dame Cathedral, standing tall and brave in the face of life's unpredictability. So, with the soul as our cornerstone, how do we build an authentic and resilient faith to flourish in a broken world?

First, trust that God is in charge of your life project, and believe the promise that all will come together for good. Find a balance between what you can control and that for which you need to lean into God for counsel. Have faith in the big plan for creation—ever evolving and love-bent.

Second, remember the part of you that was created to endure. God knows us by our souls, the essence of who we are now and forever, not fleeting hobbies, accomplishments, or appearances. The divine is in us, benevolent, luminous, and brimming with love. Dare to live from this place.

---

* See Ecclesiastes 3:11

Third, hope. To have it is critical. It will keep us participating, enduring, and helping others to do the same. Hope in all circumstances.

Fourth and finally, love is everything. You could build your whole life, a "cathedral of faith," on this one cornerstone of truth. Choose to love and be loved. Choose it again and again. It is enough.

Architect of Love,

Forgive me.
How is it that I claim we are so close,
but I haven't talked to You in days?
I take You for granted.
That is the truth.
I serve the world before my soul.
See how my ego parades.
You wait patiently for me to come to my senses.
Or—so desperate for Your mercy, Your love, Your hope
I finally lay flat at Your feet
utterly surrendered.
I in You, You in me.
It's the only way this thing called life is going to work.
When will I learn?
You are my true and faithful cornerstone.

Amen.

French Crepes

We were introduced to this simple, sweet treat by a plucky mademoiselle who set up her crepe stand next to Notre Dame Cathedral in Paris. I dream about her crepes and views of the Rose Window and gargoyles of Notre Dame all year long. It's all about balance at our house. I really want my kids to enjoy food and time around the table, which means both broccoli and Nutella make it into my shopping cart. A perfect treat at our house for breakfast, lunch, dinner, dessert, and a midnight snack is crepes with bananas and Nutella.

This is my best effort at recreating the mademoiselle's magic Stateside.

Ingredients

1 cup flour
1 ⅓ cup milk
2 eggs
2 tbsp butter, melted
2 tsp granulated sugar

1 tsp vanilla
3 bananas, thinly sliced
jar of Nutella
Powdered sugar, for dusting

Directions

In a bowl, combine flour, milk, eggs, butter, sugar, and vanilla. Either stir with a whisk or blend with a handheld blender until clumps are removed.

Choose a sauté pan that is nonstick. Add a little butter to hot pan, then spoon out a thin layer (around ¼ cup) of the batter. Roll your pan around (lifting momentarily off heat) to allow batter to cover the bottom. Cook until the edges are slightly golden.

Using a spatula, lift the crepe at the edges, then carefully flip in the pan. Cook until nicely golden brown. They cook very quickly, usually 1-2 minutes per side. Transfer the crepe to a plate and begin again with buttering your hot pan. The second crepe is always better than the first! You can stack them on a plate, because they are just as tasty warm or at room temperature. To serve, cover half the crepe with Nutella and thinly sliced banana, then flip the other half over top to fold. You can lightly dust each crepe with powdered sugar. Voilà!

44

How Big Is Your Brave?

I believe with a steadfast faith that there can never be a situation
that is utterly, totally hopeless. Hope is deeper and very, very
close to unshakable . . . To choose hope is to step firmly forward
into the howling wind, baring one's chest to the elements,
knowing that, in time, the storm will pass.
—ARCHBISHOP DESMOND TUTU

Peace I leave with you; my peace I give you. I do not give to you as
the world gives. Do not let your hearts be troubled and do not be afraid.
—JOHN 14:27 (NIV)

My grandfather was drafted into the U.S. Navy during WWII. He saw action in Pearl Harbor and in the Battle of Manila in the Philippines. "Papa JB" had one of the more daring jobs on his ship. His fellow sailors locked him into a full-body iron diving suit and then lowered him into the sea to look for mines and to repair damage to the hull suffered in battle. The kicker: My grandfather could not swim!

Imagine being dropped in the middle of the ocean in a heavy metal suit and not knowing how to swim. A terrifying prospect.

What do we do when the bottom falls out and our whole world slides off its axis? The marriage disappoints. You fall off the wagon. You lose a parent, friend, job. The doctor hands out a dreaded diagnosis. Your child is suffering. A pandemic shuts down our world.

We all will find ourselves in life situations where we don't know how to swim. I experienced such a terrible fear the day New York's Twin Towers fell five blocks from my apartment, and again a few short months later when the doctor declared, "Your son has cancer." You would think after forty-odd years on this planet, I would be somewhat competent at staying afloat. Sadly, no one is ever truly prepared for heartbreak.

Long ago, the disciple Peter experienced a similar soul shock to my grandfather, minus the iron suit. Jesus called Peter out of his boat to walk on the water toward him. He started out strong, until the winds came. Then he looked down, naturally panicked, and abruptly began to sink. Peter cried out, "Save me." Immediately, Jesus reached out his hand.

Each of us will feel the darkness press in, experience the ugly pit of fear, and endure heartbreak. Thomas Merton offers some comfort: "Perfect hope is achieved on the brink of despair, when instead of falling over the edge, we find ourselves walking on air." Hope takes spiritual grit and aid from a sacred Power much larger than ourselves or our disasters. During my son's diagnosis, there were moments when I felt like I was drowning. A still, small voice inside told me to breathe and hope. I began to swim again. Life will ask us over and over again to find our inner brave.

The promise is there. Call out—call out again, and keep calling out for God, relief will come. Pay attention to divine clues. Reach out to family, a counselor, and friends for helping hands. Make it your mission to find the light in the darkness.

Learning to entrust our lives and all we love to God is a life mission. Looking ahead, I know that with six kids, there will be many late nights where I will pace in the darkness and weep an ocean of tears. My mind, body, and spirit will be tested. I pray that you and I will not give up before God has a chance to help us climb back in the boat and reach a new and redemptive shore.

Eternal Spirit,

You are the face of the Great I Am.
You are my last muster of inner courage
when my mind, body, and spirit
want to send up the white flag of surrender.
You are the holy sacraments:
the bread, the wine, the hope
that nourish the hunger of my soul.
You are the quiet intimacy, that secret inner tug
drawing me in when the world proves cold, unmerciful.
You are the architect of miracles, small and grand.
Nothing—not time, not suffering, not loss,
not even death—
is beyond Your grace.
You are the savior of my human heart.

I humbly say Amen.

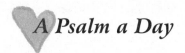

A Psalm a Day

IN MOMENTS WHEN I need an extra dose of bravery, I turn to the Psalms. I put sticky notes of the Psalms all over my apartment walls in New York when my son Charlie had cancer. They comforted me daily. The Psalms are 150 prayers and lyrical poems that cover every emotion and circumstance faced on Earth. They are so honest about what we go through as humans. For millennia, people have leaned into them for solace, wisdom, and fortitude. When we are at a loss in our prayer life, the psalms give us words. Our need of God, and God's desire to come to our rescue, is the message of the Psalms.

The following Psalms are special to me and resonate with why I love God and have reason to always hope. This week, I invite you to read a Psalm a day. If one especially touches you, write it out and tape it on your mirror, make it the background on your phone, pray it on your walks—whatever it is, let these words from Scripture bring you peace.

> **Psalm 139:1–5, 11–14:** O LORD, you have searched me and known me. You know when I sit down and when I rise up; you discern my thoughts from far away. You search out my path and my lying down and are acquainted with all my ways. Even before a word is on my tongue, you know it completely. You hem me in, behind and before, and lay your hand upon me . . . If I say, "Surely the darkness shall cover me, and night wraps itself around me," even the darkness is not dark to you; the night is as bright as the day, for darkness is as light to you. For it was you who formed my inward parts; you knit me together in my mother's womb. I praise you, for I am fearfully and wonderfully made.*

> **Psalm 91:4, 11:** He will cover you with his feathers, and under his wings you will find refuge; his faithfulness will be your shield and rampart. . . . For he will command his angels concerning you to guard you in all your ways.†

---

* NRSV
† NIV

Psalm 46:10: Be still, and know that I am God!*

Psalm 23:1–4: The LORD is my shepherd, I shall not want. He makes me lie down in green pastures; he leads me beside still waters; he restores my soul. He leads me in right paths for his name's sake. Even though I walk through the darkest valley, I fear no evil; for you are with me; your rod and your staff—they comfort me.†

*   NIV
†   NRSV

45

Plant Ground Cover

We are spiritual beings having a human experience.
—PIERRE TEILHARD DE CHARDIN

Listen! A farmer went out to sow his seed. As he was scattering the seed, some fell along the path, and the birds came and ate it up. Some fell on rocky places, where it did not have much soil. It sprang up quickly, because the soil was shallow. But when the sun came up, the plants were scorched, and they withered because they had no root. Other seed fell among thorns, which grew up and choked the plants, so that they did not bear grain. Still other seed fell on good soil. It came up, grew and produced a crop, some multiplying thirty, some sixty, some a hundred times.

—MARK 4:3–8 (NIV)

The *Biggest Little Farm* is a documentary about a California couple, Molly and John Chester, who took a daring leap to buy a parcel of parched and forgotten farmland. They spent a decade transforming it into a vibrant, biodynamic farm with miles of vegetation, orchards of fruit trees, hives of bees, chickens, cows, ducks, and pigs galore. The learning curve to create Apricot Lane Farms was steep, with significant setbacks and daily tests of patience, perseverance, finances, and faith. But there were also remarkable surprises of joy: the first fruit harvest, the success of the egg production, and the resurrection of their famous pig Emma. The journey was unpredictable, one step forward and two steps back. But through it all, the Chesters knew they were participating in something so much bigger than themselves; something beautiful, maybe even transcendent.

In the beginning at Apricot Lane Farms, the Chesters were introduced to a farmer/sage named Alan York. He gave them wonderful advice applicable to farming but also to faith: "Plant ground cover, so you are prepared for whatever is ahead." The Chesters spent most of their time and financial investment in the early years seeding their 250 acres with a massive planting of native grasses, legumes, fruit trees, and flowering vegetation. Alan York knew Apricot Lane Farms needed a deep and diverse root system for growth and protection.

Each of us has been deeded our own metaphorical farm, a plot of time and space to grow something beautiful and benevolent with our lives. We must make sure we have deep enough roots to sustain us through life's unpredictable setbacks. God's desire is for us to flourish—budding in every season, in every field of our lives. Father Thomas Keating wrote, "It is never too late to start the spiritual journey or start over, and it is worth starting over any number of times." The vitality of my "farm" depends on my rootedness in the things that give my life deep meaning: my faith, my relationships, and my work. I bear fruit when I am cultivating peace within, peace with others, and peace in the larger world. I measure successful seasons in my life by my resilience, inner joy, and capacity to hope.

The reality, of course, is there will be seasons when our faith isn't yielding the quantity or quality of fruit we would like. We will feel disconnected from our inner spiritual self and God. The truth, as detailed in Jesus' Parable of the Sower, is that sometimes our "farms" are full of rocks, thorns, and weeds. The life of faith will always be a work in progress. We are "sacred imperfections." Our job is to hold on to the divine thread through the thicks and thins of life, and try our best to keep our hearts open to grace. What I love about this parable is whatever the season or condition of one's faith, from now into eternity, God never stops sowing seeds. He'll throw grace on the rocky soil, the thorn patches, and fields overgrown with weeds. God never gives up on us. He is a God of unrelenting hope and radical grace. God is confident new buds will come.

After many years of crippling drought in California, a deluge of rain set in, dropping more than eighteen inches of rain in a single twenty-four-hour period. The topsoil of all the neighboring farms washed into the ocean. They were ruined. But not Apricot Lane Farms. The years of planting diverse ground cover with deep roots had protected the farm from this natural disaster.

In your life, you should expect and prepare for precarious weather on your metaphorical farm; floods, droughts, and plagues are part of every faith story. Laying spiritual ground cover will be our salvation.

You can lay your ground cover in an infinite number of creative ways. Set your table and offer fellowship to friends, family, and strangers. Be spiritually open and porous. Set aside time for quiet and meditation. Read the Bible. Pray without ceasing. Nourish your soul in nature. Find a purpose for your life that is larger than yourself. Get healthy and strong for any uphill battle. You don't build the farm overnight. Do a little each day, and one day you will relish the reward of your efforts.

Loving God,

It was You who planted the idea of heaven
in my heart first.
Yet evil persists.
I weary from gripping the thread of hope
so tightly in my hands.
Help me stay the path.

Yesterday, I watched a mother cardinal
dressed in her taupe plumes
working on her nest, one twig at a time.
Could this be the cure for my inner tremble?
Keep building my nest—my life?
One twig at a time,
connecting the dots for goodness,
mining the darkness for light,
daring to love,
trusting You,
convinced that one day
I will see:
You were with me all along!

A grateful Amen.

Turkey Chili

Every Saturday, I head to the Farmer's Market to hunt for the "crop of the season." A farm-to-table meal is a blank canvas on which to be creative with the farmer's bounty and prepare a meal to serve many. A mother of six, I am also all about a one-pot meal. I love an all-day simmering pot of chili on the stovetop because it makes my kitchen smell delicious. This chili is full of flavor and can feed my family for days.

All my soups and stews start with a classic mirepoix, the fancy French word for sautéing carrots, onions, and celery with piquant spices. It's up to you how many beans and the degree of spice. I usually do lentils, white beans, black beans, or red kidney beans. My favorite thing about this recipe are all the chopped fresh herbs thrown into the pot at the end. Why not make it delicious as well as healthy?

Ingredients

olive oil
1 cup onion, diced
1 cup carrots, diced
1 cup celery, diced
salt and pepper
1 tsp chili powder
1 tsp cumin
1 tsp turmeric
½ tsp cinnamon
1 lb ground turkey breast
2 (28 oz) cans whole tomatoes
2-3 cups chicken stock or water
3 tbsp tomato paste
1 red bell pepper, diced, seeds and ribs removed
1 yellow bell pepper, diced, seeds and ribs removed

1 orange bell pepper, diced, seeds and ribs removed
1 green bell pepper, diced, seeds and ribs removed
1 cup sweet potatoes, cut in chunks
1 cup French lentils (I like the sprouted green ones!)
1 (14 oz) can cannellini, red kidney, or black beans, rinsed (or more, per your taste!)
1 tbsp brown sugar
1 cup cilantro, chopped
1 cup Italian parsley, chopped
1 cup spinach, chopped
juice from 1 lime

Directions

Coat the bottom of your pot generously with olive oil. Sauté your onion, carrots, celery, salt, pepper, and spices until soft. Add ground turkey breast. Once turkey meat is cooked through, pour the cans of tomatoes (including liquid), chicken stock, and tomato paste into the pot. Add your peppers, sweet potatoes, and lentils. Allow to simmer for at least 30 minutes, and longer if you have the time. Next add your beans. Taste all along the way. I usually cut up the tomatoes in the pot and end up adding more spices! At this point, you may add the sugar to reduce acidity. The cilan-tro, parsley, and spinach are my healthy twist on the chili. I stir in the greenery at the very end—a beautiful accoutrement!

The fun part of a chili dinner at our house is the toppings: a squeeze of lime, a heaping tablespoon of diced avocado, a spoon-ful or two of grated cheese, a dollop of Greek yogurt, and some tortilla chips. Kids love it.

46

Something More

The fullness of joy is to behold God in everything.
—JULIAN OF NORWICH

"I have seen the Lord!"
—MARY MAGDALENE, JOHN 20:18 (NIV)

Last summer, I made a pilgrimage to a cave in the Massif de la Sainte-Baume mountains in the south of France. Mary Magdalene, a spiritual heroine of mine and a prominent part of the Christian story, spent her final years supposedly attended by angels in this grotto. Accompanied by my eldest son, Charlie, and youngest son, Finn, we joined a group of fellow pilgrims on the steep footpath, *Le Chemin des Roys,* or "the Kings' Road."

I set my kids free to discover the recesses of the cave on their own while I sat quietly before the statue of Mary of Magdala. Curious about this woman who was a member of Jesus' inner circle, I imagined the conversations she must have shared with him on their travels. Mary likely heard him preach the Beatitudes, saw him heal the blind and the lepers, and witnessed his invitation to so many to begin a new life with him. Mary knew his unique, humble manner and maybe even what Jesus liked to eat, what made him laugh, rise in anger, or shed a tear. She had a front-row seat to the miracles and also painfully experienced the completion of his earthly destiny. Mary Magdalene knew Jesus had changed our world forever. She glimpsed heaven brought to Earth. What must it have felt like to be that close to God?

Sadly, for over 1,400 years we lost the story of this brave, heroic, intimate friend of Jesus—Mary of Magdala. In the sixth century, Pope Gregory the Great and the larger Church launched a campaign to diminish the role of women in Jesus' life and ministry. The pope preached three sermons blurring the story of Mary Magdalene with that of the sinful woman found in the gospel of Luke. The damage was done. Fake news apparently is not a modern phenomenon!

Thanks to recent theological scholarship and the archeological discovery of the noncanonical Gospel of Mary in 1896, we have reclaimed the true Mary, an independent woman of financial means who was very important to Jesus. She was devoted to his ministry both during and certainly after his crucifixion and resurrection. Pope Francis has acknowledged the Church's wrongs and bestowed on Mary a High Feast Day (June 22). He elevated her to an equal standing with the male apostles.

Since my pilgrimage experience, Mary Magdalene has taken on a more important influence in my spiritual life. It is meaningful to me that Jesus included a woman in his inner circle and entrusted her with his divine personhood and holy work. It is inspiring that Jesus appeared to Mary first after his resurrection. I like to think it was because of her distinctly feminine faith and her unfailing devotion to him and his mission. The other disciples fled in fear and self-protection. Mary Magdalene never left Jesus' side. Steely, she stood beneath the cross and endured what must have been devastatingly hard so that Jesus would know he was not alone. Her bravery made an impact and resonates with me today.

I desire the faith of Mary. Mary Magdalene gives me courage when my first instinct is to run and hide from the hard and heartbreaking. She trusted her soul's intuition that God is offering us something more here on Earth. She knew that a deep and sacred existence, where love is the reason for everything, could be her reality and ours too. Our daily lives offer ample opportunities to witness grace-at-work here and now. We can experience "God come to Earth" just as Mary did. The moment we believe God is real and present in our daily lives, the ordinary does become something more, surprisingly holy. Every time that I bless, feed, forgive, heal, delight, laugh, hope, and love, Jesus comes near. And I glimpse a little of what Mary must have experienced in his presence, heaven brought to Earth.

Holy and Loving God,

Into the wilderness I go.
The path is unknown
but the destination is certain.

You make beautiful things out of dust.
May this be a season of uncovering
the spark of You within the dust of me,
my eyes opened for the sacred in the imperfection.

Some days the direction is unclear,
my questions find no answers,
my prayers are met with silence,
fear nestles under my breastplate,
and the Dark wraps itself around me.
Come then.
Be my beacon.

Help me make peace with
my doubts and brokenness, even my end.
Hold my hand through the whole of it.
I'd like to have the "faith of Mary."

A hopeful Amen.

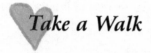

Take a Walk

He joins me in my ramble. Divides abode with me. No friend
have I that so persists as this Eternity.
—EMILY DICKINSON

Mary Magdalene and Jesus must have taken many walks together. I imagine this is where she learned about the heart of God and the potential of her own heart in the process. I was introduced to the British concept of taking long countryside walks when I lived in London for graduate school, and it has since become a way for me to draw closer to God and take the measure of my own heart. My husband and I were invited by a classmate to join her family on a weekend walk in the English countryside. The Brits sometimes refer to these daylong excursions crossing through pastures, over river streams, and through forests as a *ramble*. Like Emily Dickinson, I too have felt Jesus on my rambles in nature.

It is scientifically proven that walking increases creativity and is the best form of exercise for the mind and the body. I hope you will experience the grace of a ramble too.

Try this beautiful chant to find your solace.

A Navajo Walking Meditation

With beauty before me, may I walk.
With beauty behind me, may I walk.
With beauty above me, may I walk.
With beauty below me, may I walk.
With beauty all around me, may I walk.
Wandering on the trail of beauty, may I walk.

47

À La Bonne Franquette

No mean woman can cook well. It calls for a generous spirit,
a light hand, and a large heart.
—EDEN PHILLPOTTS

Give me your heart and let your eyes delight in my ways.
—PROVERBS 23:26 (NIV)

It was 6:00 P.M. on a lovely summer evening. I received a phone call
from my new friend Lise saying that she and her husband, Eric, would
love to stop by. Always up for any opportunity to gather people around
my table, without a second thought, I answered an enthusiastic, "Yes!"
Next, I called my neighbors Lotte and Jerry and invited them to join us
too. When I got off the phone, my husband, David, said, "How are you
going to feed everybody?"

Oh, my. I had just invited two French-trained chefs, Eric and Lise. Both
had worked in Michelin-starred restaurants in Paris, and currently ran a
very popular French bistro. What could I serve? I opened the refrigerator
to find a bag of lettuce, a handful of figs from David's tree, one avocado, a
block of Parmesan, a container of dried apricots, some nuts, left over
croissants from breakfast, cold cheese pizza, an apricot tart, and my
birthday cake (which had Finn's five-year-old fingerprints all over it). And
the pièce de résistance: a single bar of dark chocolate!

I certainly was not going to be the Hostess with the Mostest. And as
luck would have it, the power went out halfway through the preparations.

I pulled a quilt from the hall closet and arranged a collection of candles in odd shapes and rainbow colors. I took an ancient French baker's wooden kneading board, bought as a wall decoration, and proceeded to assemble a smorgasbord of nuts, dried fruit, and sliced figs stuffed with blue cheese and drizzled with honey. I smeared Nutella on the toasted croissants (which my kids loved for dinner!) and turned a baguette into avocado toast. I whipped up one of my salads with cherries, Parmesan, fresh mint, basil, olive oil, vinegar, and honey from the garden. I narrowly sliced what remained of the apricot tart and topped it with vanilla gelato and grated dark chocolate!

Eric strolled into the kitchen to find me in my apron, flushed and sheepish. My first words were "I am sorry!!" He greeted me cheek to cheek with a kiss, smiled, and presented from behind his back a bottle of wine and a paper sack full of homemade blueberry muffins. "No worries," he said. "These are my favorite evenings, spontaneous, with people *just happy to be together*. We open our cupboards, empty our refrigerators, open wine long overdue for a special occasion, and the night somehow becomes *magic*. Welcome to À La Bonne Franquette!"

I handed Eric a stack of paper napkins and we just laughed together. He carried the sheet-pan pizza that I had tried my best to upgrade with olives and arugula. We both smiled at the group of new and old friends gathered around the candlelit table enjoying the buffet of "everything but my kitchen sink." We laughed. We told stories. We toasted each other. We happily took turns passing around their sleeping baby. It was a perfect evening!

There was no need for a three-star beef bourguignon or a starched white tablecloth and embroidered napkins when we had a sky of stars, flickering candles, and genuine smiles. Here lies the secret recipe for living a life that shines with meaning and spills with joy: Make the ordinary moments sacred, even holy. Choose presence over perfection. Some of my most memorable meals had little to do with what was served and everything to do with how we felt seen, included, and loved.

Jesus was the master of *à la bonne franquette*. He knew how short our time is here, how precious each moment together. Jesus asks us to be present, not perfect. Take what we have to offer, the simple and ordinary, and use it for good. Do you remember what Jesus did with a loaf, a few fish, and a carafe of wine? He set a simple table for those he loved. But what transpired around that gathered table was transcendent. Two thousand years later, we still hunger for the same thing: unconditional love, sure hope, and infinite mercy. I am convinced that Jesus set that table as a model so that one day we might serve as hosts at our own "tables of love." Homemade sourdough or animal crackers, Châteauneuf or grape juice—it doesn't matter, only that love is shared.

Let's follow Jesus' lead and show this hurting, broken world what joy looks like again. The next time you're tempted to turn down an invitation to break bread with others, don't give your regrets. Instead, open up your cupboards, pull up more chairs to your table, and love well who is right in front of you!

Dear God,

Thank you for the daily sacraments that make life holy:
chopping vegetables, baking bread,
gathering together,
walking through a forest of pines,

planting parsley, mint, and thyme,
listening to my seven-year-old read Dr. Seuss,
holding my husband's hand,
dancing in the kitchen,
finding a heart rock,
and the whispering of prayers, many.

A very grateful Amen.

Love in a Bowl

Food and time spent around the table provides the most marvelous stage for love and laughter, grieving and healing, blessing and growing. The kitchen table is the "heart" of my life. Cooking is my love language. I welcome any opportunity to pull out my favorite tablecloth, scatter candles of all shapes and sizes down the center, arrange a couple of mason jars of flowers, and feed family, friends, and strangers. Meaningful life happens here. I have always been a free-spirit hostess, barefoot in the kitchen, Indigo Girls playing in the background, and kids everywhere. Don't be surprised if you find yourself drinking wine out of a Spider-Man birthday paper cup. All that matters is that you feel special when you take your seat at my table.

In the spirit of an *à la bonne franquette* kind of evening, I love to set up a smorgasbord of ingredients for friends and family to make my favorite Love in a Bowl. With various dietary restrictions, allergies, and tastes, every guest is happily set free to make a bowl of love that's perfect for them. Everyone loves an invitation to be creative. I will prepare in advance a couple grains (black rice, farro, pasta, or couscous), some protein options (grilled chicken, roasted salmon, lentils, and boiled eggs), a variety of salad greens and fresh herbs, a platter of roasted vegetables with lots of chopped fresh basil, mint, and parsley. I love to offer an assortment of roasted nuts (hazelnuts, walnuts, almonds, and toasted pumpkin seeds), an olive medley, dried and fresh fruit options, and lots of yummy cheeses (Parmesan, Manchego, and feta!). And don't forget fresh slices of avocado, wedges of lemon or lime, and a really good balsamic and olive oil. Count the smiles!

Ingredients

2 sweet potatoes, washed and chopped like French fries
2 fennel bulbs, washed and sliced at an angle
2 heads of broccoli, chopped
1 cup cherry tomatoes, halved
1 cup Portobello mushrooms, washed and halved
2 bell peppers (red, green, orange, or yellow), sliced into strips
olive oil
kosher salt
½ cup Parmesan, grated
1 cup fresh Italian parsley, chopped
ground black pepper
2 cups forbidden (black) rice
4 cups water

1 tbsp grass-fed butter
1 cup dried Montmorency cherries
½ cup fresh mint, chopped
2 tbsp honey
1 cup roasted nuts, chopped (Marcona almonds, walnuts, hazelnuts)
1 cup Parmesan ribbons (shaved using a vegetable peeler)
6 salmon fillets
1 tbsp herbes de Provence
1 bag fresh spinach
1 shallot, diced
1 garlic clove, whole and peeled
1 cup blackberries
2 avocados, sliced

Directions

Following is one of my favorite love bowls: black rice, roasted salmon and vegetables, sautéed spinach, and avocado.

Preheat oven to 425°F for vegetables and salmon. Cover one or two sheet pans, depending on how many vegetables you would like to roast, with parchment, and arrange vegetables so they have space to breathe. Drizzle an abundance of olive oil over vegetables, followed by kosher salt, cracked pepper, and grated Parmesan. Roast until crisp. Squeeze lemon, a little extra Parmesan, and a scattering of fresh parsley.

Prepare black rice; set aside to cool. Stir butter into rice, with dried cherries, parsley, mint, honey, and hazelnuts. Salt and pepper to taste.

Wash and pat dry your salmon fillets. Dress each with olive oil and a thick coating of herbes de Provence, salt, and pepper. Lay the flesh side down on the sauté pan and cook for 2-3 minutes. You are aiming for a crusty surface. Next, flip the salmon, transfer the entire sauté pan to the oven, and cook for 5-8 minutes.

Sauté your diced shallot and clove of garlic in olive oil until fragrant, then add your fresh spinach, tossing for 1-2 minutes. Season with fleur de sel and fresh-ground pepper.

Set out a collection of fun bowls for your guests. Invite them to create their own love bowl. For my bowl, I start with sautéed spinach and black rice, topped with a salmon fillet. I decorate the edges of the bowl with roasted vegetables, tuck in sliced avocado and ribbons of Parmesan. I toss in a handful of fresh herbs (basil, parsley, mint), fresh blackberries, toasted Marcona almonds, then drizzle with olive oil, a swirl of balsamic vinegar or a squeeze of lemon, kosher salt, and fresh-ground pepper. Voilà!—love in a bowl!

48

A Divine Edit

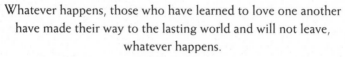

Whatever happens, those who have learned to love one another
have made their way to the lasting world and will not leave,
whatever happens.
—WENDELL BERRY

Above all, be loving. This ties everything together perfectly.
—COLOSSIANS 3:14 (GW)

My mom is my trusted critical reader of my first thoughts penned to paper. She has a gift for trimming unnecessary verbiage to reveal the heart of my message. A sentence especially liked will be underlined a couple of times for emphasis. Sometimes she will even write in the margin, "Beautifully said." It is a true lesson in humility to watch a hard-won sentence suffer the fate of her razor-sharp pencil. And yet the result is always better for it.

Language is unique and beautiful to humans. It allows communication, direction, and healing. Your words matter. All the adjectives, adverbs, nouns, and verbs form the sentences that not only tell our significant stories but change opinions, inspire greatness, offer solace, and set us free.

My favorite words are:

wonder
mystery

mercy
friend
delicious
pray
walk
glow
laugh
magnanimous
resilient
chocolate
hope
dream
love

That last one is the King of Words.

But then there are the negative ones that clutter the page, cause stress, and hurt us and others:

resent
hurt
ignore
anger
jealous
fear
destroy
bitter
anxious
greed

despair
cruel
hate
exclusive
inferior

These words stop us in place, stunt our growth, and diminish—even destroy—the magic of any story.

With the gift of free will, God allows us to write the chapters of our lives, hopefully to fit beautifully into the larger, divine story. Many of the words have no place but the cutting-room floor. Sometimes, practicing self-awareness, we catch them ourselves and erase them before they are inked on our life's page. Others need a firm but compassionate edit. Thankfully, God is not afraid to strike a red line through our pride and prune those emotions that harm us. The divine edit always makes us stronger.

Communication is God's gift to us. Honor it. Show compassion when addressing others and especially yourself. The power of hateful words is truly greater than the cut of a swinging sword. Positive criticism is the only kind. Reflect on the impact of your words for the evil or good they leave behind. Use your words to lift a spirit, not diminish it.

Every so often we receive a double underline, a "Well done" scribbled in the metaphorical margin, or a couple of excited exclamation marks, which let us know we have written something worthy with our lives.

This week be gentle with yourself and others. Remember that life is in a constant state of creation and revision. I believe God is regularly helping us edit our lives down to one word: *love*.

Dear God,

Thank you for being the Editor of my life.
Edit me down to one word: Love.
Cut out all the unholy verbiage.
Ex out worry, fear, bitterness—
they take away from my story.
Let my pages be filled with
wonder and thankfulness.
Red-line the negative emotions
and expectations that do not serve me.
Give me new words—
Bold, brave, and radiant are good ones.
They describe who You created me to be.
Make my story worth telling.

Amen.

Sticky Note Challenge

My kindergartner is learning to read. Every Monday, his teacher sends home a list of new sight words that he is to commit to memory. He writes them down on pink, yellow, blue, and green sticky notes and then we tape them all over the house, from the refrigerator door to the kitchen counter to his bathroom mirror, even to the front door for a laugh.

Compose a list of words that you would like your week to be about. Write them down on sticky notes and tape them all over your house for inspiration. Not only will they be glory reminders to you, but also to everyone who crosses your threshold! This week, my words are *hope, courage, light,* and *laugh*. What are yours?

49

Big Kahuna

We have to be braver than we think we can be, because God is
constantly calling us to be more than we are.
—Madeleine L'Engle

Suffering produces endurance, and endurance produces character, and
character produces hope, and hope does not disappoint.
—Romans 5:3–5 (NRSV)

"When you hit the Big Kahuna, dig in, paddle harder," yelled Shane, our shaggy-haired, sun-burnished adventure river guide. He knelt at the stern of our raft as we entered the class 3 rapid called the Big Kahuna on the Snake River in Jackson Hole. This was my first experience of whitewater rafting, and I was not prepared for this mighty, thrashing beast. Before we stepped into the six-person inflatable yellow raft, Shane explained what excitement we could expect over the next two hours on the river. He enthusiastically described the assortment of wildlife, the superior heights and speeds, and the awesome beauty of the river. It was only while checking our life preservers that he casually mentioned strong paddling was our best bet for staying *in the boat* when the raft entered the challenging rapids.

Have you ever paddled through class 3 rapids? Or looked up and seen a ten-foot wall of water on all sides? Wondered if the tiny rubber blow-up raft could survive what life was throwing your way? Turns out Shane did not know just how much wisdom I found in his call from the stern of the raft: "Dig in, paddle harder."

Much like a river, life proves mightily unpredictable. We leisurely float, suffer some bruises, maybe a rock or a tree stump temporarily blocks our passage, or the current takes us off in a direction we didn't expect or desire. Big Kahunas are part of every story. Sometimes in life and on the river, you just have to put your head down and keep paddling, believing smooth waters are ahead.

It wasn't until I was twenty-eight that I experienced my first Big Kahuna of life's rapids. When my son was diagnosed with cancer, I did all the wrong things at first. I panicked. I got angry. I yelled at God standing at the helm of my boat and fought like hell to paddle backward, anything to return to my life before the rapids. The "paddle" of my tender faith seemed inadequate at first to see me through. It was my mom who stood up in the center of my boat and volunteered to paddle for me when I had no strength left. You can't go through rapids on your own.

Smooth waters are pleasant, but we find out who we truly are when we dig in and paddle through the rough waters. The greatest surprise on the river and in life is when we finally reach the flats, worn and weary, and realize we made it through. We are in calm waters again. When we are inside the hole of the Big Kahuna rapid, we forget that joy may only last for a while, but pain, too, is temporary. It's all part of this unpredictable and yet tremendously sacred story of the river, of life itself. Dig in!

Loving God,

The clouds come, the sky darkens.
The waves cut through my courage.
The wind—so malevolent.

No rainbows in sight.
I am now an unmoored soul.
I am afraid, God.
Then Your voice rises up in me:
"All things are possible, little boat,
if you believe."
I take back hold of my courage
and head into the rapids,
cresting hard with hope.
When the morning finally comes,
my boat is battered indeed.
But what a story to tell—
about this little boat who trusted
and prevailed.

Amen.

Ranger Cookies

This recipe means more than its measurements of flour, butter, oats, and chocolate chips. When we were faced with the Big Ka-huna of my son's devastating cancer diagnosis and yearlong treat-ment, my aunt Jen would weekly mail a tin of these cookies from South Carolina to my New York City apartment building. Even the doormen knew they were like manna from heaven. I can promise you these cookies buoyed my heart and helped me dig in, paddle harder! And bonus: They are delicious and easy to make! If you don't like raisins, or chocolate or walnuts, leave them out and substitute with an ingredient you do like!

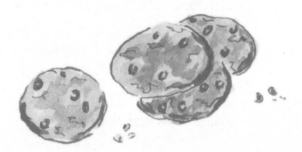

Ingredients

1 cup grass-fed butter, softened
½ tsp kosher salt
1 tsp vanilla
1 cup turbinado sugar
2 eggs
1 cup light brown sugar

2 cups flour
1 tsp baking soda
2 cups oats
1 cup raisins
1 cup walnuts, or nut of your choice
2 cups dark chocolate chips

Directions

Preheat oven to 350°F. Cream butter until soft. Add salt and vanilla. Add turbinado sugar and eggs (one at a time), beating with a fork. Mix well. Add brown sugar. Sift flour and baking soda into wet ingredients. Mix in oats, raisins, nuts, and chocolate chips. Drop dough by tablespoon onto parchment-covered baking sheet. Bake for 12–15 minutes. Lay on wire racks to cool. Enjoy!

50

Recipe of Faith

I paint the pattern of joy in your heart and leave it for you to find.
—ARCHBISHOP DESMOND TUTU

And the peace of God, which transcends all understanding,
will guard your hearts and your minds.
—PHILIPPIANS 4:7 (NIV)

Any French chef will proudly tell you that a roux (flour, clarified butter, and special seasoning) is the foundation of every classic French recipe. A good roux promises a memorable dish, ensures depth, and has an intoxicating aroma and velvety richness. The inspired chef knows when a roux needs another bay leaf, a dash of smoky paprika, or a hot chili pepper to elevate the flavor.

Cooking is a beautiful metaphor for faith. The recipe of my faith is grounded in a belief in the Divine, whom I know as God, Jesus, healer, friend, and model for how to live and love. After that, there are infinite creative ways to flavor and enhance one's personal spiritual experience. There is a French culinary expression, cooking *au pif*, which roughly translated means cooking "by the nose," or being led by one's intuition. The French would say you can literally "taste the heart" of a chef who creates recipes *au pif*. They are curious, take risks, and follow their heart to create a dish that is transcendent. A faith that grounds us and gives us wings is guided by the intuitive soul. We have to listen to and be guided by the "still, small voice of God" within.

You will know when your inner spiritual "roux" needs a little seasoning. Feelings of self-doubt, regret, and fear spar within your heart. Maybe we are listening more to the world than to our intuitive souls. Sprinting the hamster's wheel, your days turn into weeks, those weeks turn into months, and one day you wake up and have lost touch with yourself and with God. Sometimes—like Emeril Lagasse, the New Orleans chef—we have to "kick it up a notch" to invigorate our faith.

My recipe for a hearty faith includes the ingredients of time spent in candlelit chapels, walks in nature, quiet times in prayer, reading and studying the Bible, and giving compassionately to others. I have also seasoned my own spiritual roux with pilgrimage visits to holy sites, participation in a faith community, and practicing meditative yoga. But I've found that the simplest ingredient is just plain quietude.

Stillness is the most underrated and yet crucial ingredient in any spiritual roux. It's humbling what transpires in the silence. Quiet truths, not meant for anyone else, surface in the absence of noise. Truths about oneself and God. Inevitably, in the silence, confessions spill from the heart. And God responds with a poetry of benediction. In a world that is loud and geared for 24/7 activity, it is a challenge to be still and listen for God. I try to begin each day with moments of stillness. At the very least, I experience a softer landing to my day, my crooked edges mysteriously smoothed out.

Inner peace, regardless of external circumstances, is a goal worth pursuing. So, too, is a willingness to be curious and dare new ingredients to enhance and deepen the recipe of your faith.

Tie on your apron and kick it up a notch!

Holy and Loving God,

I imagine it's deliciously quiet in heaven.
Finally, nothing stands in the way of the soul
hearing the Beloved's enlightened words.

Sometimes I glimpse Your peace beyond understanding.
The art is in learning how to live there.

Usually, I have to retire from the cacophony of my life,
humbled, to turn in.
It's up for grabs if my soul can get past the ego
guarding the entrance into the Holy of Holies.

I can thank the breath and whispered prayers for
pointing the way.
One slow inhale, one slow exhale.
One slow, Be still. One slow, And know that I am God.

Not every time, but sometimes I slip past the veil,
and I know something of heaven.
Lush and supple on the inside, only love.

When will I learn?
The fight-or-flight cycle ages me,
where the stillness makes me immortal.

One slow inhale, one slow exhale.
One slow, Be still. One slow, And know that I am God.
I return through the veil with the scent of hope on
my skin.

Amen.

Breath Meditation

We . . . are being kept in being by the very breath of God
from moment to moment.
—ARCHBISHOP DESMOND TUTU

Thomas Merton proclaimed, "The gate of heaven is everywhere." Breath meditation leads us out of the noise and into a sanctuary of quiet where God feels real and near. Inner peace is possible. The soul revives in the stillness.

To practice stillness, try this simple breathing exercise. I call it my Darth Vader breathing, or ocean breath. You should hear the sound of your breath in your ears, like listening to the ocean through a conch shell. Tongue rests at the roof of the mouth. Mouth is closed. Breathe through your nose three counts, as if you are moving up a staircase, hold it at the top, and then release the breath through your nose at the same measured pace coming down the staircase to three counts. Sometimes it is helpful for me to set a goal number of breaths, such as thirty, before I can settle into my skin and experience true stillness. The reward is that the world receives a gentler, more hopeful version of me. And my soul has what it needs to embrace the fullest human spiritual existence possible.

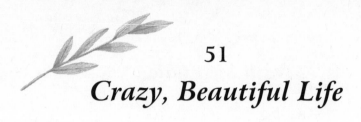

51
Crazy, Beautiful Life

The glory of God is a human being fully alive.
—St. Irenaeus

He has set eternity in the human heart.
—Ecclesiastes 3:11(NIV)

There are certain human beings who by gift, miracle, or courageous choice embody a spirit far larger than their bodies can hold, a spirit so full that we would find their DNA shimmering on the fabric of any soul blessed to cross their paths. We all want to know who we are, why we are here, and what is our unique purpose. The people who know it are easy to spot: Their lives shine with meaning.

The word *sentient* appeared in an op-ed essay in the Sunday *New York Times*. The writer was the well-known neurologist and author Oliver Sacks. He wrote in response to learning he had a terminal illness: "I have loved and been loved . . . I have read and traveled and thought and written . . . Above all, I have been a sentient being . . . on this beautiful planet, and that in itself has been an enormous privilege and adventure."

I was struck by the line "Above all, I have been a sentient being." I googled this mysterious word. Eighteenth-century philosophers made the distinction between one who is controlled by reason (rational) and one who is guided by intuition (sentient). Another definition describes a sentient being as one who lives the "conscious life," fully engaged in the human spiritual experience.

The sentient are determined to accomplish a soulfull life. They plunge body, mind, and soul headlong into life, determined to smell, taste, see, and especially love until the end, whatever the cost. They perceive the world as enchanted. Less interested in oneself, they are fascinated by other people, delighted and intrigued by their stories. Heartbreak, disappointment, and loss are mined calmly for meaning. Resentment of ill fortune is just not allowed, because the sentient are focused on the chance to participate again. This curious, excited sojourner has learned to see life for all its potentialities and knows the stay is much too short.

Jesus gives us permission to live a crazy, beautiful life. He declares, "I came so you would have life, and life in all its fullness."*

I knew a Mr. J, who was determined to live a crazy, beautiful life. He climbed every mountain peak in North America, skied double black diamonds, built his own telescope to see the stars, ran a marathon in the rain, enjoyed Mozart, Bach, and Beethoven and the operas of *Tosca, Carmen,* and *La Bohème.* He took up black-and-white photography and cooked pancakes with his sons at the local homeless shelter on Sunday mornings in the winter. He attempted to grow orchids and was an avid reader of history. He was also a beloved local doctor who was just as interested in healing the spirit as the body. I met him at the end of his life. Thankfulness was his constant mantra. He died very peacefully, having lived and loved to the nth degree. The sentient know all is a gift.

Do not be afraid to fully engage in your human experience. So much is missed when we try to protect ourselves from emotional discomfort. Re-

---

* John 10:10, GNT

member it is in the challenging moments that our eyes are opened to new possibilities and hidden rewards. For those who live in Nashville, country music lyrics become beloved mantras. One of my very favorites by Tim McGraw, "Live Like You Were Dying," sums up the mission. There is no time to wait.

This week, cultivate sentience. Be guided by gratitude and curiosity. Meet the world less from that rational brain, more from your heart. Indulge the senses, follow your intuition, do what makes your soul happiest. Welcome to a crazy, beautiful life.

Dear God,

Faith is my declaration:
I am on the side of Love.
It is my arms wide open to life.
It is my response to a world come undone,
rolled up sleeves, fists in the air,
fighting for heaven on Earth.
It is my daily resistance to despair.
Ultimately, faith is my decision to trust You,
with all that I am and love.
Humbly, I pray for the gift of more breaths,
more experiences of beauty,
more relationships that enrich,
more highs than lows,
more tempests and even more rainbows—

I still have much to learn about myself,
about You,
and how Love makes this planet turn.

Amen.

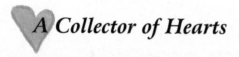

A Collector of Hearts

The most beautiful things in the world cannot be seen or touched,
they are felt with the heart.
—ANTOINE DE SAINT-EXUPÉRY

I have always loved the shape of a heart. Several years ago, my daughter Elise and I began hunting them on our nature walks. We have a beautiful collection of smooth river stones, shells, and turquoise sea glass hearts on the bookshelf. We also take pictures of heart-shaped clouds, cactus plants, rock formations, leaves, and even the spicy pepperoni on our Friday night pizza. When we email or text a photo of our latest heart find, it's like we are sending each other a love note!

I see them everywhere now. I don't think it's a coincidence when I find a leaf in the shape of a heart while jogging at Radnor Lake or pluck a juicy, heart-shaped tomato off the vine for my mozzarella salad. Maybe it's the universe's way of reminding me love is the reason for everything!

We are called by the Creator to collect hearts, an activity of a true sentient. Now, I am not talking about heart-shaped river rocks or clouds in the sky, but actual human hearts. The sentient know that we are not put on this Earth for ourselves alone. Our lives must serve a greater good. We live in a world where many are hurting and long to be seen and loved. And we can do that for one another. A crazy, beautiful life is only possible if we help make it possible for another. George Eliot wrote, "Blessed is the influence of one true, loving human soul on another."

You will know you've touched a human heart because your very own heart will be touched. This week, look for hearts everywhere. Rocks, leaves, clouds, even your pepperoni slice. Let them remind you that Love is your mission.

52

Never Postpone Joy!

Joy is the serious business of Heaven.
—C. S. LEWIS

"You shall go out in joy and be led back in peace; the mountains
and the hills before you shall burst into song, and all the trees of
the field shall clap their hands."
—ISAIAH 55:12 (NRSV)

J oy is an experience of transcendence. It happens when the soul—that
most beautiful, divine part of you—catches a glimmer of heaven.

People filled with this souljoy are mysteriously lit from the inside out.
They glow. Even when all around them is darkness and uncertainty, they
have an incredible gift of locating joy. They aim higher, for a more holy
experience of living here on Earth. They have learned a great life lesson:
Never postpone joy!

One of my favorite discoveries has been *The Book of Joy: Lasting Happiness in a Changing World,* by the Dalai Lama and Archbishop Desmond
Tutu. This 380-page love letter offers a surprisingly intimate, endearing,
often humorous revelation of two of the most remarkable spiritual leaders of our time. The authors reflect on the secrets to finding joy in all circumstances, even, and especially, in suffering.

The Dalai Lama lived for fifty-six years in self-imposed exile from his
home, family, and kingdom. Archbishop Tutu endured years of terror,
imprisonment, and violence in his fight against apartheid in South Africa.

Many times, either of them could have taken an easier route and raised the white flag of surrender. Instead, they held fast to a "dogged sense of hope," trusted that redemption would come, and chose joy over despair. They compiled a list of secrets to practicing joy in all circumstances. My top three are perspective, humor, and generosity.

To experience regular joy, we must address our fears. Anxiousness is a joy-killer. Laughter is spiritual relief. Deep and abiding joy is rooted in a belief that life is a privilege. The soul sits at the edge of her seat eager for any opportunity to drink in beauty, experience love, and extend or expand hope. God wants us to be a people of joy. Jesus did not disappoint. He relished the beauty and peace found in nature. He savored friendships and enjoyed a good party. He found deep joy in fighting for justice and lifting up people. Ultimately, he could abide in joy in all circumstances because he absolutely believed in God's powerful love for him.

Archbishop Desmond Tutu reminds us that we are "loved with a love that nothing can shake . . . And God wants us to be like God. Filled with life and goodness and laughter—and joy!"

The Dalai Lama proclaimed: "Every day is a new opportunity to begin again!" That is my new mantra. Every day I should try to experience a little bit of heaven here on Earth. You and I accomplish joy not in isolation but together. The fastest way to reach joy for ourselves is to make it possible for another.

Dear God,

Joy is my sacred mission.
Herein lies my work.
I am saved in the saving.

Maybe long after I am gone,
when perhaps You and I
share the same address,
or You have sent me off
on another grand adventure,
it will be said,
"Her little puzzle piece mattered."

Amen.

Love Muffin

It could be written on my tombstone: She made a really great muffin! These muffins are special because I created them for my best friend after she was diagnosed with celiac disease, and now they are famous because I've kept the recipe secret until now! My friend has a sweet tooth, and I was determined to create a healthy treat that she could relish for both breakfast and dessert. Friends have been known to show up unannounced at my door to sneak a couple for afternoon-pickup rounds, and I regularly make surprise love drops of my muffins to friends and family for whom I want to show a little extra love and spark joy.

Ingredients

2 cups oat flour
1 cup almond meal
1 ¼ tsp baking soda
½ tsp kosher salt
1 cup turbinado sugar

7 ripe bananas, smashed
1 cup coconut oil, melted
2 tsp vanilla
1 cup dark chocolate chips
   (more if desired)

Directions

Preheat oven to 350°F. In one bowl, mix together oat flour, almond meal, baking soda, and salt. In another bowl, combine sugar, bananas, coconut oil, and vanilla. Mix and then marry the two bowls! The coup de grâce: chocolate—the more, the better in my book. And it's proven that dark chocolate is good for the brain—and a smile! Fold in the dark chocolate chips to the batter; reserve a handful of chocolate chips to decorate the tops of the muffins before baking. Line a muffin tin with paper liners, fill each muffin cup, and bake 20 minutes. For an extra-moist muffin, take them out a little earlier. Straight out of the oven, split your muffin and smear with almond butter. Joy complete!

More Soulfull Nourishment

The gift of a blessing for your table and a few more of my favorite recipes.

Dear God,

Bless this table,
family and friends around,
bring laughter abundant,
encouragement aplenty,
trespasses forgiven,
new possibilities born,
hope received for another day,
our bodies and souls marvelously full.

Amen.

A Twist on Spaghetti

I have my mom to thank for this delicious recipe, and for always encouraging me to keep adding new ingredients to my spiritual repertoire. There are no Michelin stars for a bland recipe or bland faith. Both in the kitchen and in the quiet of my heart, I have to taste-test which spices will reward with a vibrant dish and a spiritual life. Cooking and faith become a fun adventure when we dare to spice it up! My mom's special riff on traditional spaghetti does not disappoint! Serve with a green salad and cheesy garlic bread.

Ingredients

1 whole organic chicken
½ onion
1 stalk of celery
1 Parmesan rind (optional)
1 bay leaf
sea salt and ground pepper
1 green pepper, diced
1 onion, diced
1 stalk of celery, diced
1 tbsp butter or olive oil
½ lb white mushrooms, sliced
2 (28 oz) cans whole tomatoes, with juice

1 can (8 oz) tomato paste
1½ tsp turbinado or brown sugar
1 tbsp olive oil
1½ cups chicken stock
½ cup red or white wine (your preference)
1 tbsp herbes de Provence
2 tsp oregano
2 tbsp capers
1 jar artichoke hearts, drained
1 cup Parmesan, finely grated
1 lb spaghetti noodles

Directions

Cook whole chicken in a pot of salted water with ½ onion, stalk of celery, bay leaf, Parmesan rind (optional), salt, and pepper for 45 minutes. You will use the chicken and the homemade stock in the recipe. Set aside to cool. Debone the chicken, reserve 1½–2 cups of your chicken stock, and then freeze the rest. I shred the white meat to use in this meal and reserve the legs and thighs for my husband's lunch! If you are in a pinch, you can use store-bought chicken stock and a rotisserie chicken.

In a large pot, begin a mirepoix by sautéing your green pepper, onion, and celery in butter or olive oil until translucent. Add your mushrooms and sauté until tender. Next, add your tomatoes and juice, tomato paste, sugar, homemade chicken stock, wine, herbs, shredded chicken, and salt and pepper to taste. Cook for 15 minutes. Add your capers and artichoke hearts and cook until slightly tender. Pour in half the Parmesan and reserve the rest for topping the spaghetti. Salt and pepper to taste.

In a separate pot, bring your salted water to boil and cook the spaghetti to al dente. At our house, we serve straight from the stovetop, a pile of noodles topped with the sauce and a spoonful or two of grated Parmesan for good measure!

Mama's Green Soup!

If you were to ask any Michelin-starred French chef (a culinary genius of foie gras, pâté, truffles, and the perfect chocolate soufflé) what they prepare for themselves and their families off the clock and barefoot in their own kitchens, they wouldn't think twice: an omelet or a purée! My children call this recipe Mom's Green Soup. The French call it a purée, which is just a fancy way of saying a vegetable soup that has been blended smooth to perfection! I love this soup because I can slip lots of worthy green vegetables into the pot that otherwise would have gotten the thumbs-down from my six-year-old! This soup is velvety in texture and boasts the most exquisite emerald color! The beauty of the recipe is that there is almost no fancy chopping, because everything hits the blender at the end. You can happily garnish with ribbons of Parmesan, cracked pepper, toasted almonds, or my homemade rosemary-olive croutons.

Ingredients

2 leeks, cleaned of sand and roughly chopped
2 carrots, peeled and diced
1 onion, roughly chopped
4 stalks celery, washed and roughly chopped
olive oil, butter, or coconut oil
1 tbsp herbes de Provence
salt and pepper
1 bouquet garni (2 bay leaves and a couple sprigs fresh thyme tied in twine for easy removal)
1 rind Parmigiano-Reggiano
3 Idaho potatoes, washed, peeled, cut in quarters

1 quart chicken or vegetable stock, and if need be, an additional cup or two of distilled water
2–3 large zucchini, or 1 package baby zucchini, washed, skin on, roughly chopped
1 large bag fresh spinach
2 10-oz bags fresh or frozen English peas
1 cup Italian parsley, chopped
1 cup Parmigiano-Reggiano, grated
swirl of olive or truffle oil

Directions

In the family soup pot, sauté your mirepoix of leeks, carrots, onion, and celery in olive oil, butter, or coconut oil. Add a tablespoon of herbes de Provence, salt, and pepper. Once the onions are translucent, add bouquet garni, Parmigiano rind, potatoes, and chicken stock, and simmer until your potatoes are soft. Turn off the heat and fold in zucchini, spinach, peas, parsley, and grated cheese, and let simmer for a couple of minutes. The beauty of the soup is that it retains its bright-green color. Green vegetables should be al dente. Remove Parmigiano rind and bouquet garni. Transfer soup to the blender and purée until perfectly smooth. Add salt, a swirl of olive oil or truffle oil, and fresh-ground pepper. Garnish with Parmigiano, croutons, and toasted almonds. Split a baguette in half open-faced on a baking sheet, butter it, sprinkle your favorite cheese and a little kosher salt and pepper, and toast until crisp.

Ribollita Soup

The stomach is an excellent way to the heart. My favorite way to show love is to arrive at the doorstep of a friend, family, or church member with my robin's-egg blue Le Creuset soup pot and a smile. Warm, healthy, homemade vegetable soup sets off a domino effect of healing. Every Italian *nonna* (grandmother) knows this recipe by heart. My marvelous vegetable and white bean soup will nourish body and soul.

Ingredients

1 extra-large yellow onion, diced
2 leeks, washed and trimmed
2 cups carrots, diced
2 cups celery, diced
1 bulb fennel, chopped
high-quality olive oil
1 tbsp herbes de Provence
kosher salt and ground pepper
1 bay leaf
1 Parmesan rind
2 (28 oz) cans whole tomatoes
12–14 cups vegetable* or chicken stock

1 cup French Le Puy lentils
1 cup shredded Savoy cabbage
2 cups fresh spinach, chopped
1 cup fresh basil leaves, chopped, plus more for garnish
½ cup Italian parsley, chopped
4–5 cups kale, coarsely chopped
1–2 cans cannellini beans
2 cups sourdough bread cubes (no hard crusts)
1 cup Parmesan, grated, plus more for garnish

Directions

In a soup pot, sauté your mirepoix of onion, leeks, carrots, celery, and fennel with generous olive oil, herbs de Provence, bay leaf, and salt and pepper until soft. Add Parmesan rind, tomatoes, stock, and lentils. Allow to simmer for 30 minutes. Once the lentils are soft, toss in your greens. Turn off heat and stir. Blend half the white beans with a little stock and a swirl of olive oil, then fold into the soup with remaining beans. Stir in your

cubes of sourdough; or, if you prefer, top soup with homemade sourdough croutons. Pour in grated Parmesan and stir. Use more cheese and
basil to garnish the soup. Salt and pepper to taste. The soup gets even
better the next day! Accompany with a simple green
salad (arugula) with Parmesan ribbons (shaved using
a vegetable peeler), olive oil, lemon juice, and
kosher salt. Don't forget the crusty
bread and dishes of olive oil for
dipping.

Lavender Madeleines

The poet Mary Oliver said, "Joy is not meant to be a crumb!" I am a huge believer that it is the little things that give us joy! Hot out of the oven, these buttery masterpieces are certain to turn any frown upside down. The beauty of the recipe is you can add chocolate, orange blossom water, or culinary lavender. They are all delicious to dunk in a mug of hot chocolate.

Ingredients

1 Madeleine mold baking sheet
1 stick plus two tablespoons
    unsalted butter
juice from 1 lemon
½ tbsp lemon zest
3 large eggs, room temperature
1 large egg yolk, room
    temperature

1 cup granulated white sugar
½ tsp kosher salt or fleur de sel
1½ cups all-purpose flour, plus ¼
    cup for dusting pans
1 tsp baking powder
1 tbsp lavender buds (optional)
powdered sugar, for dusting

Directions

Melt butter over low heat and then stir in lemon juice and zest. In either a standing mixer or using a mixing bowl with hand mixer, combine the lemon butter, eggs, yolk, sugar, and salt. Beat until mixture is smooth and has a ribbonlike consistency. Fold in 1½ cups flour and 1 teaspoon baking powder. If you are using lavender buds, you can either fold them into the batter now or sprinkle them on top after baking. Cover your batter and refrigerate for 2 hours. Preheat oven to 375°F. Prepare your Madeleine baking sheet with either melted butter or coconut oil, dusted with flour and placed in the refrigerator until baking time. Spoon batter into each Madeleine mold, then bake 6–8 minutes. Allow to cool. Gently tap the Madeleines from the tray, dust with powdered sugar, and serve warm.

Acknowledgments

Sissy Gardner, it is because of you that *Soulfull* came into being! Remember the day in the bookstore when you said, "Farrell, we need a book like this. Go write it!" Thank you and thanks to Parnassus Books for continuing to champion me as an author!

Is it even possible to thank Karen White, my mom and editor extraordinaire? Her fingerprints are all over this work of love. I could not have done it without you, nor anything else in my life. You make everything better.

Margaret Riley King, a friendship of almost twenty years. The truth is, if you have Margaret in your corner, you have more than won. Thank you for believing in me. All of this is because of you!

Becky Nesbitt, the wait was worth it! You have blessed me with the most incredible life-giving, dream-fulfilling writing experience with you as my editor and champion. You are generous and kind, and you have made me a better writer. Not to mention, this has been so much fun. I just want to create with you again and again.

Leita Williams, I love working with you. You are in the sacred thick of it; the book is better for having your mind and heart invested in it.

Thank you to production editor Jocelyn Kiker, copy editor Lara Kennedy, proofreader Julia Henderson, and designer Virginia Norey for transforming my manuscript into a book that I am proud of. Infinite gratitude to Convergent!

Morgan Stone, the book is blessed by all your meaningful contributions.

Thank you to Clay Stauffer and Woodmont Christian Church—if only everyone could be blessed with a leader and church home as supportive and loving!

Blanca, you are my forever sous-chef and guardian angel. There is no way to express my gratitude for how you continue to love and bless my family!

What an incredible blessing to have friends like Anne, Ashley, Dorothy, Elizabeth, Jamee, Jody, Kemp, Mel, Sarah, and Tallu who make me laugh, support me in the valleys, and sit on the front row cheering my victories.

I have Victor Judge, Vanderbilt professor, writer, and incredible human being, to thank for being my mentor, and for helping me pursue my passion for the arts and theology. Thank you for introducing me to Flannery O'Connor, Rainer Maria Rilke, Gerard Manley Hopkins, Emily Dickinson, and so many other "artist theologians" who have deepened my faith and inspired my writing.

This book would not have been possible without the creative genius, hard work, and determination of Laura Deleot. She has been my friend and cheerleader start to finish.

Evie Coates, you radiate soulfulness in your art and in your life. What a coup to have you create the cover for *Soulfull!*

Thank you to Kathryn Birkholz for the beautiful illustrations.

To Maime and Pops, your generosity, love, and devotion to our family are astounding. I have you to thank for introducing me to Provence and Jackson Hole, the setting for so much of my writing and joy.

I have my five sisters, Mahaley, Mary Carlisle, Belle, Harrison, and Ramsey, and my mom and dad to thank for blessing me with a foundation of love (and fun!).

My taste-testers (even the green pea soup!), cheerleaders, and the reason my life is large, deep, and so full of joy: Charlie, Belle, Elise, Rose, Percy, and Finn—this is my three-hundred-page love letter to you!

And finally, and most importantly, I thank David, my soulmate, for daring this wild, loud, and crazy soulfull adventure with me. Six kids, four dogs, ducks, bees, and hopefully a peacock in our future. You love me the way every person should be loved in this world.

Farrell's Favorites

Books

A Book of Hours by Thomas Merton

Cold Tangerines by Shauna Niequist

An Altar in the World by Barbara Brown Taylor

What We Wish Were True by Tallu Schuyler Quinn

Living Buddha, Living Christ by Thich Nhat Hanh

Letters to a Young Poet by Maria Rainer Rilke

Rilke's Book of Hours: Love Poems to God by Rainer Maria Rilke

Love Poems from God by Daniel Ladinsky

The Remarkable Ordinary by Frederick Buechner

Devotions by Mary Oliver

The Alchemist by Paulo Coelho

Mere Christianity by C. S. Lewis

Anam Cara by John O'Donohue

Beauty by John O'Donohue

The Return of the Prodigal Son by Henri Nouwen

The Universal Christ by Richard Rohr

Consolations by David Whyte

The Book of Joy by Archbishop Desmond Tutu and 14th Dalai Lama

Music

"The Four Seasons" by Antonio Vivaldi

"Agnus Dei" by Samuel Barber

The Piano (music from the motion picture)

"Für Elise," "Ode to Joy" by Ludwig van Beethoven

"Oceans," "So Will I" by Hillsong

"Goldberg Variations" by Johann Sebastian Bach

"Closer to Fine" by The Indigo Girls

"Shepherd Moons," "Caribbean Blue" by Enya

"I Still Haven't Found What I'm Looking For," "40" by U2

"Light of the World," "Trust in You," "Thank God I Do" by Lauren Daigle

"Riser" by Dierks Bentley

"So Will I (100 Billion X)," "Oceans" by Hillsong United

Cookbooks

The Cook's Atelier by Marjorie Taylor and Kendall Smith Franchini

Summers in France by Kathryn M. Ireland

French Country Cooking by Mimi Thorisson

The Forest Feast by Erin Gleeson

My Paris Kitchen by David Lebovitz

The Little Paris Kitchen by Rachel Khoo

Plenty by Yotam Ottolenghi

The Barefoot Contessa Cookbook by Ina Garten

Seasons by Donna Hay

Love & Lemons by Jeanine Donofrio

Film & Television

Chef's Table

My Octopus Teacher

The Biggest Little Farm

Podcasts

Turning to the Mystics with James Finley

On Being with Krista Tippett

Soulful 7 Conversations with Farrell Mason

Soulfull Citations

Epigraph

Buechner, Frederick. *Now and Then: A Memoir of Vocation*. HarperOne, 1991.

Introduction

Oliver, Mary. "The Summer Day." *House of Light*. Beacon Press, 1992.

1: Build Your Nest

Bailie, Gil. *Violence Unveiled: Humanity at the Crossroads*. Herder & Herder, 1986.

Brooks, Arthur. *From Strength to Strength: Finding Success, Happiness, and Deep Purpose in the Second Half of Life*. Portfolio Penguin, 2022.

Fox, Matthew. *Meister Eckhart: A Mystic-Warrior for Our Times*. New World Library, 2014.

Hugo, Victor. *Les Misérables*. Simon & Schuster, 2005.

Oliver, Mary. "Starlings in Winter," *Owls and Other Fantasies: Poems and Essays*. Beacon Press, 2006.

Zera, Richard. *Business Wit & Wisdom*. Beard Books, 2005.

2: Finding Eden

Shrady, Maria. *Angelus Silesius: The Cherubinic Wanderer*. Paulist Press, 1986.

3: Live in Hope

Safford, Victoria. "The Gates of Hope." Stanford Social Innovation Review. ssir.org/articles/entry/the_gates_of_hope.

4: When Heaven Breaks Through

Dillard, Annie. *Pilgrim at Tinker Creek*. Harper Perennial Modern Classics, 1998.

Whitman, Walt. *Leaves of Grass*. Modern Library, 2000.

5: Earning Feathers

O'Connor, Flannery. *The Habit of Being: Letters of Flannery O'Connor*. Farrar, Straus and Giroux, 1988.

Rohr, Richard. "Gazing Upon the Mystery." Center for Action and Contemplation. Oct. 21, 2018. cac.org/gazing-upon-the-mystery-2018-10-21/.

6: Two Stones

Dostoevsky, Fyodor. *The Brothers Karamazov*. Farrar, Straus and Giroux, 2002.

7: Your Life Is Your Prayer

Taylor, Barbara Brown. *An Alter in the World: A Geography of Faith*, HarperOne, 2010.

8: "No Mud, No Lotus"

Kübler-Ross, Elisabeth. *Death: The Final Stage of Growth*. Scribner, 1997.

Thich Nhat Hanh. *Living Buddha, Living Christ*. Rider, 1996.

9: The Secret Life of Bees

Dickinson, Emily. *Poems: Second Series*. Edited by T. W. Higginson and Mabel Loomis Todd. Roberts Brothers of Boston, 1891.

10: *It's a da Vinci*

Blostein, Denise, Robert Libetti, and Kelly Crow. "How a $450 Million da Vinci Was Lost in America—and Later Found." *The Wall Street Journal.* Sept. 19, 2018. wsj.com/articles/fresh-details-reveal-how-450 -million-da-vinci-was-lost-in-americaand-later-found-1537305592.

Peterson, Eugene. *The Message.* NavPress, 1993.

11: *Roll with It*

Vande Kappelle, Robert P. *Walking on Water: Living Into a New Way of Thinking.* Wipf & Stock Publishers, 2020.

12: *Lighten Your Pack*

Buechner, Frederick. *The Remarkable Ordinary.* Zondervan, 2017.

Mackesy, Charlie. *The Boy, the Mole, the Fox, and the Horse.* HarperOne, 2019.

13: *One Square Inch of Silence*

Gamalinda, Eric. "The Properties of Light." *Zero Gravity.* Alice James Books, 1999. soundtracker.com/about-gordon-hempton

14: *Waiting*

Holmes, Oliver Wendell. *Over the Teacups.* Leopold Classic Library, 2016.

15: *Lay Down Your Stones*

Coelho, Paulo. *By the River Piedra I Sat Down and Wept: A Novel of Forgiveness.* Harper Perennial, 2006.

16: *Tree Hugger*

WABC-TV. "In rare handwritten note, Martin Luther King Jr. reveals what he thinks is the meaning of love." *Eyewitness News,* ABC7 NY,

Feb. 10, 2020. abc7ny.com/mlk-day-martin-luther-king-junior-jr/
5917393/.

Wohlleben, Peter. *The Hidden Life of Trees*. Greystone Books, 2016.

17: Cut a New Destiny

van Gogh, Vincent. "Letter from Vincent van Gogh to Theo Van
Gogh; 10 October 1882." webexhibits.org/vangogh/letter/11/
238.htm.

Matisse, Henri, and Jack D. Flam. *Matisse on Art*. University of
California Press, 1995.

18: Eyes Peeled

Dickinson, Emily. "Some Keep the Sabbath Going to Church."
The Complete Poems of Emily Dickinson. Edited by Thomas H. Johnson.
Back Bay Books, 1976.

Hopkins, Gerard Manley. "God's Grandeur." *Gerard Manley Hopkins:
Poems and Prose*. Penguin Classics, 1985.

19: Ready to Fly

Buechner, Frederick. *The Magnificent Defeat*. HarperOne, 1985.

Mother Teresa and Brian Kolodiejchuk. *Mother Teresa: Come Be My Light*.
Penguin Random House, 2003.

20: Press On

For the full text of St. Patrick's breastplate prayer, see irishcentral
.com/roots/st-patricks-breastplate-prayer-irelands-patron
-saint.

21: Go to the Well

O'Donohue, John. *Anam Cara: A Book of Celtic Wisdom*. Harper
Perennial, 1998.

22: *Walk as if You Are Kissing the Earth with Your Feet*

Thich Nhat Hanh. *Being Peace*. Parallax Press, 2005.

Thich Nhat Hanh. *Living Buddha, Living Christ*. Rider, 1996.

Thich Nhat Hanh. *The Miracle of Mindfulness: An Introduction to the Practice of Meditation*. Beacon Press, 1999.

Thich Nhat Hanh. *Peace Is Every Step: The Path of Mindfulness in Everyday Life*. Random House, 1992.

23: *More Wonder!*

Browning, Elizabeth Barrett. "Aurora Leigh." *The Oxford Book of English Mystical Verse*. The Clarendon Press, 1917.

O'Donohue, John. *Beauty: The Invisible Embrace: Rediscovering the True Sources of Compassion, Serenity, and Hope*. Harper, 2004.

Tozer, A. W. *The Pursuit of God*. Loki's Publishing, 2017.

24: *Who Takes the Lead?*

Brooks, David. *The Second Mountain: The Quest for a Moral Life*. Random House, 2020.

Quinn, Tallu Schuyler. *What We Wish Were True: Reflections on Nurturing Life and Facing Death*. Convergent, 2022.

25: *It's an Inside Job*

Milne, A. A. *Winnie-the-Pooh*. Ishi Press, 2011.

26: *Not Another PB&J*

Moore, Thomas. *Care of the Soul: A Guide for Cultivating Depth and Sacredness in Everyday Life*. Harper Perennial, 2016.

27: *Lions, Tigers, Bears, Oh My!*

Baum, L. Frank. *The Wizard of Oz*. Puffin Classics, 2019.

Coffin, William Sloane. *Letters to a Young Doubter*. Westminster John Knox Press, 2005.

28: Keep Casting!

Barks, Coleman. *The Soul of Rumi. A New Collection of Ecstatic Poems.* HarperOne, 2002.

29: The Journey of the Soul

Dickinson, Emily. Johnson "Because I Could Not Stop for Death." *The Complete Poems of Emily Dickinson.* Edited by Thomas H. Johnson. Back Bay Books, 1976.

Quinn, Tallu Schuyler. *What We Wish Were True: Reflections on Nurturing Life and Facing Death.* Convergent, 2022.

30: Hope Does Not Disappoint

Tippett, Krista, host. "Mary Karr: Astonished by the Human Comedy." *On Being* (podcast). October 13, 2016. onbeing.org/programs/mary-karr-astonished-by-the-human-comedy-jan2018/.

Sagan, Carl. *The Cosmic Connection: An Extraterrestrial Perspective.* Dell, 1975.

ten Boom, Corrie. *The Hiding Place.* Bantam Books, 1974.

Dickinson, Emily. "Not Knowing When the Dawn Will Come." *The Complete Poems of Emily Dickinson.* Edited by Thomas H. Johnson. Back Bay Books, 1976.

31: New Ribbons

Dickinson, Emily. Johnson "I Dwell in Possibility." *The Complete Poems of Emily Dickinson.* Edited by Thomas H. Johnson. Back Bay Books, 1976.

Mackesy, Charlie. *The Boy, the Mole, the Fox and the Horse.* HarperOne, 2019.

Rilke, Rainer Maria. *Letters to a Young Poet.* W. W. Norton & Company, 1993.

32: *What I Know to Be True*

Nouwen, Henri. *The Return of the Prodigal Son: A Story of Homecoming.* Image, 1994.

van Gogh, Vincent. "Letter from Vincent van Gogh to Theo Van Gogh; 3 September 1882." Van Gogh's Letters. webexhibits.org/vangogh/letter/11/228.htm.

33: *Don't Be a Tourist in Your Own Life*

Thoreau, Henry David. *Walden.* Empire Books, 2012.

34: *The Little Way*

Thérèse of Lisieux. *The Story of a Soul: The Autobiography of St. Thérèse of Lisieux.* TAN Books, 2010.

35: *One Flat Tire*

O'Donohue, John. *Beauty: The Invisible Embrace: Rediscovering the True Sources of Compassion, Serenity, and Hope.* Harper, 2004.

Faulkner, William. *The Sound and the Fury.* Vintage, 1990.

36: *Green Is My Color*

Berry, Wendell. "Manifesto: The Mad Farmer Liberation Front." *The Country of Marriage.* Counterpoint, 1971.

37: *Follow Your Bliss*

Campbell, Joseph. *The Power of Myth.* Anchor, 1991.

Morrison, Toni. "College Commencement Address." Wellesley College, 2004.

Pressfield, Steven. *The War of Art.* Rugged Land, 2002.

Waldrop, Mitch. "Inside Einstein's Love Affair with 'Lina—' His Cherished Violin." *National Geographic,* Feb 3, 2017. national geographic.com/adventure/article/einstein-genius-violin-music -physics-science.

Bailie, Gil. *Violence Unveiled: Humanity at the Crossroads.* Herder & Herder, 1986.

38: Kintsugi

Merton, Thomas. *A Book of Hours.* Sorin Books, 2007.

39: How Much for a Hug?

Blake, William. "The Little Black Boy." *Songs of Innocence.* Dover Publications, 1971.

Coelho, Paulo. *Aleph.* Vintage, 2012.

40: Faith Gazing

Taylor, Barbara Brown. *An Altar in the World.* HarperOne, 2009.

41: Jenga

Fox, Matthew. *Christian Mystics, 365 Readings and Meditations.* New World Library, 2011.

McCabe, Herbert. *God Still Matters.* Continuum, 2002.

42: What Truly Matters

Berry, Wendell. "Manifesto: The Mad Farmer Liberation Front." *The Country of Marriage.* Harcourt Brace Jovanovich, Inc., 1973.

Levertov, Denise. *Denise Levertov: Selected Poems.* New Directions, 2003.

Nepo, Mark. *Inside the Miracle: Ending Suffering, Approaching Wholeness.* Sounds True, 2015.

Oliver, Mary. "The Summer Day." *House of Light.* Beacon Press, 1992.

Quinn, Tallu Schuyler. *What We Wish Were True: Reflections on Nurturing Life and Facing Death*. Convergent, 2022.

Rilke, Rainer Maria. "Go to the Limits of Your Longing." *The Book of Hours: Prayers to a Lowly God*. Northwestern University Press, 2002.

43: Your Cornerstone

MacSwain, Robert, and Michael Ward, eds. *The Cambridge Companion to C. S. Lewis*. Cambridge University Press, 2010.

44: How Big Is Your Brave?

Bochen, Christine M., Patrick F. O'Connell, and William H. Shannon. *The Thomas Merton Encyclopedia*. Orbis Books, 2006.

Tutu, Desmond, and Dalai Lama. *The Book of Joy*. Cornerstone Publishers, 2016.

45: Plant Ground Cover

The Biggest Little Farm Documentary. FarmLore Films, LLC (Sandra Keats), 2018.

Keating, Thomas. "The Human Condition: Contemplation and Transformation." *The Harold M. Wit Lectures*. Harvard University Divinity School, 1997. invialumen.org/uploads/3/7/5/4/37541063/the_human_condition_contemplation_and_transformation_by_father_thomas_keating.pdf.

Winfrey, Oprah. *What I Know for Sure*. Flatiron Books, 2014.

46: Something More

Dickinson, Emily. "The Blunder Is in Estimate." *The Complete Poems of Emily Dickinson*. Edited by Thomas H. Johnson. Back Bay Books, 1976.

Wordsworth, William. "Resolution and Independence." *Poems, in Two Volumes*. Broadview Press, 2015.

47: À La Bonne Franquette

Phillpotts, Eden. *The Portreeve*. Methuen & Co., 1906.

48: A Divine Edit

Berry, Wendell. *Given*. Counterpoint, 2006.

49: Big Kahuna

L'Engle, Madeleine. *Walking on Water: Reflections on Faith & Art*. Bantam Books, 1982.

50: Recipe of Faith

Tutu, Desmond, and Mpho Tutu. *Made for Goodness and Why This Makes All the Difference*. HarperOne, 2010.

51: Crazy, Beautiful Life

de Saint-Exupéry, Antoine. *The Little Prince*. Mariner Books, 2000.

Eliot, George. *Scenes of Clerical Life*. Bibliotech Press, 2020.

Sacks, Oliver. "My Own Life." *The New York Times*, Opinion. Feb. 19, 2015.

52: Never Postpone Joy!

Lewis, C. S. *Letters to Malcolm: Chiefly on Prayer*. Mariner Books, 2002.

Tutu, Desmond, and Dalai Lama. *The Book of Joy*. Cornerstone Publishers, 2016.

Resources for Living Soulfully

Index | Recipes

Index | Spiritual Reflections

About the Author

FARRELL MASON is a writer, spiritual blogger, host of the *Soulful 7 Conversations* podcast, and mother of six children. She is the author of two works of fiction, *Alma Gloria and the Olive Tree* and *The Angel and the Raven*, as well as a collection of prayers, *The Pocket Cathedral*. She holds a master of art and business from The University of Manchester and a master of divinity with a concentration in theology and the arts from Vanderbilt University. She is a part-time ordained minister of pastoral care at Woodmont Christian Church in Nashville.

Farrell Mason's great joy is found barefoot and making mischief in the kitchen with her family and friends, eating a croissant in Paris, or hiking in the Tetons. Her heart is forever committed to raising funds and awareness for kids with cancer, in honor of her son. In all of her writing, you will find a thread of hope, healing, and redemption.

breadandhoneyblog.net
youtube.com/@soulful7conversations796
Instagram @breadandhoneyblog
booktok @living.soulfully

About the Type

This book was set in Albertina, a typeface created by Dutch calligrapher and designer Chris Brand (1921–98). Brand's original drawings, based on calligraphic principles, were modified considerably to conform to the technological limitations of typesetting in the early 1960s. The development of digital technology later allowed Frank E. Blokland (b. 1959) of the Dutch Type Library to restore the typeface to its creator's original intentions.